How to draw
Vintage Fashion

Celia Joicey &
Dennis Nothdruft

How to draw
Vintage Fashion

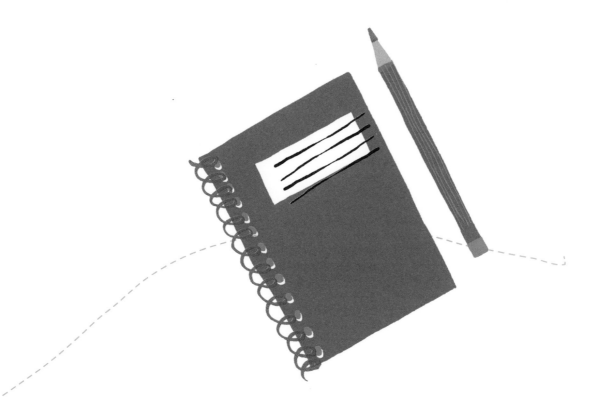

Thames & Hudson

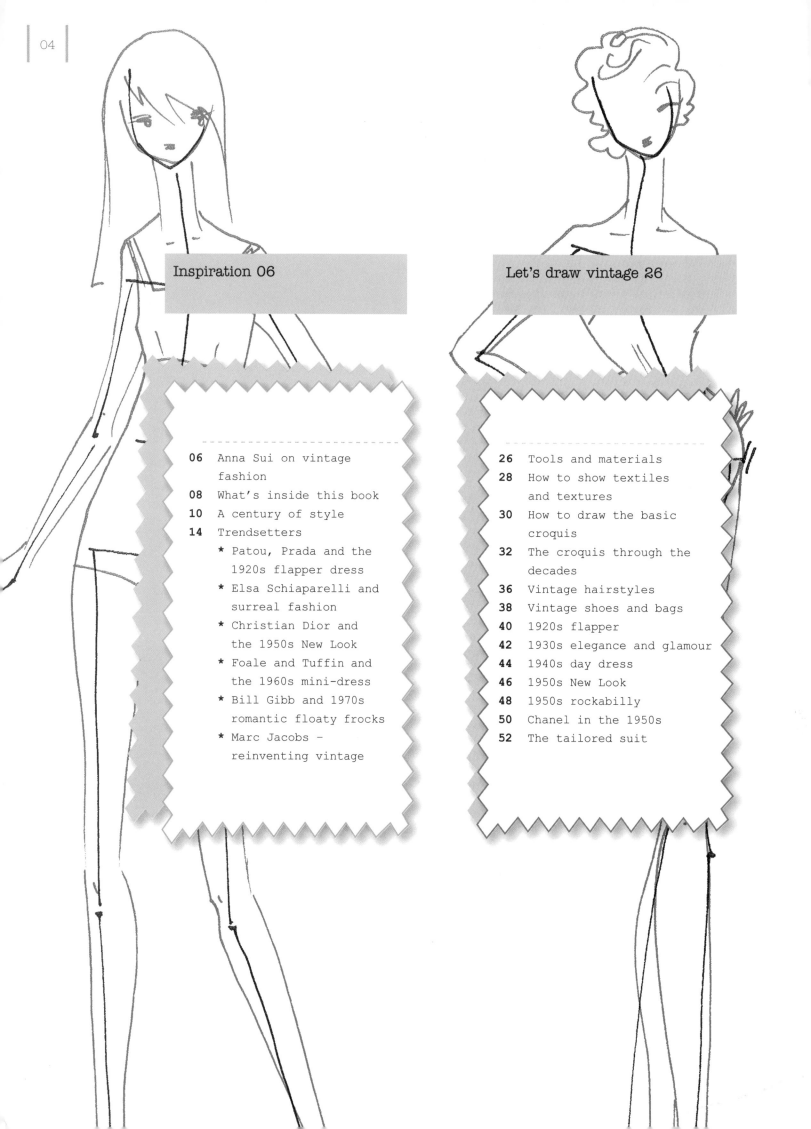

Inspiration 06

Let's draw vintage 26

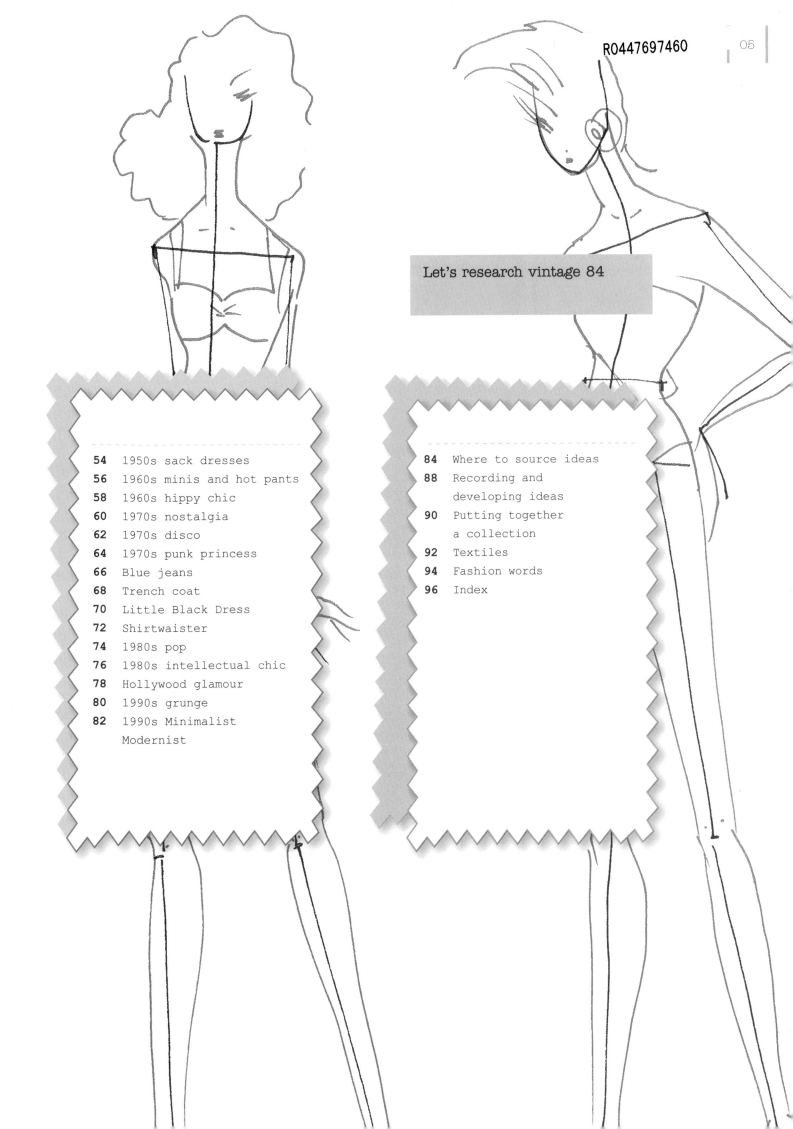

Let's research vintage 84

Hello, my name is Anna Sui. I'm a fashion designer, and I love vintage! History was always my favourite subject in school. I love **doing research** and learning about something new. I like to take my audience on that journey with me, to be as inspired as I am. When I was working on my own book, I looked at a lot of other designers' books, and I was sometimes puzzled why they didn't share their inspirations. It's the multitude of **ideas underlying the work** that I think most people find interesting. I always like to know the thought process behind a collection.

I love going to **flea markets**, especially when I am travelling, because I love seeing the 'stuff' of other cultures – **handicrafts** and things with **historical content**. I love the whole story behind why something happened when it did. That's what I try to put into my own collections.

I think **the 1960s** was the period that really shaped me and my love of fashion. To me, that decade always seems like a time of ultimate optimism. Everything was changing – music, film, design, art – and there was a feeling of revolution, freedom and infinite possibility. Going back in history, my **favourite fashion designers** are Paul Poiret, Léon Bakst, Coco Chanel, Rudi Gernreich, Mary Quant, Marimekko, Yves Saint Laurent, Ossie Clark and Zandra Rhodes. I also am always inspired by what Barbara Hulanicki did with her shop Biba in the 1960s.

In my own design career I've done collections **inspired by many different looks** – Edwardian dandies, Bloomsbury writers, Pre-Raphaelite painters, rococo gypsies, Victorian cowboys, French New Wave cinema, the Russian Ballet … Sometimes I mix up **styles from different periods and cultures**. The inspiration for one of my collections began with the French queen Marie Antoinette. Then, on a trip to Istanbul, I discovered the romance of Turkish pirates. I had also seen a documentary about the band, the New York Dolls (with their strict dress code of black, red and white … with stripes, stars and roses). I **put all these elements together**, including printed textiles based on tiles at Topkapı Palace in Istanbul. The result was my Pirate Collection.

I hope that you will enjoy looking at all the different vintage styles on the pages that follow, and that they will give you all the inspiration you need to create your own designs.

The outfit above left shows a strong Oriental influence, while the outfit above right includes typical 1960s features. The four figures on the right come from Anna Sui's Pirate Collection.

So you want to draw vintage?

This book introduces you to some of the
key looks that fashion designers have
created over the decades. Be inspired
by the sections on *Trendsetters, Let's
draw vintage* and *Let's research vintage*.

Trendsetters

In this section, experts on vintage
fashion including famous designers,
models and fashion photographers
choose their favourite key looks –
the trendsetting designs that have
helped to shape fashion over the
decades.

Study the photographs and
drawings and read the text to learn
about the designers behind these
trends, and to discover why the
looks they created are so important
in the history of fashion.

Take inspiration from the designs
and use them to create your own
vintage-style looks. Remember to
keep your sketches so that you can
refer back to them.

Read what the
professionals say
and learn about each
trendsetting look

Original
drawings
and photos

When you see the
names of designers you
don't know, look them
up. Do you like their
styles?

Get ideas for
where to do your
research and find
inspiration

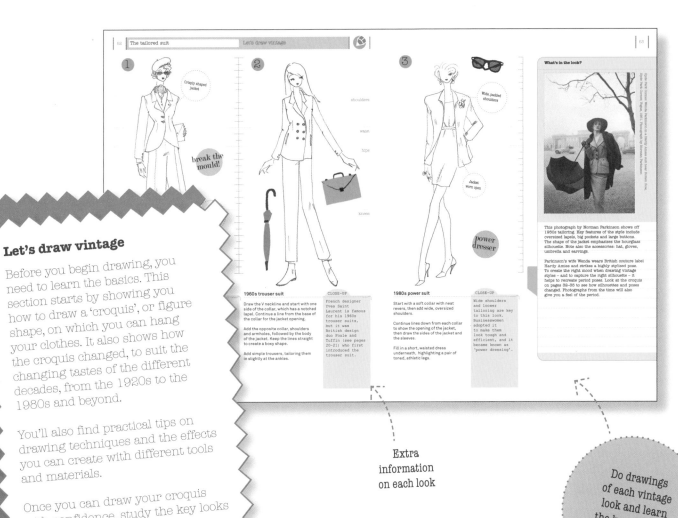

1 Crisply shaped jacket

break the mould!

2 shoulders

waist

hips

knees

power dresser

3 Wide, padded shoulders

jacket worn open

What's in the look?

This photograph by Norman Parkinson shows off 1980s tailoring. Key features of the style include oversized lapels, big pockets and large buttons. The shape of the jacket emphasises the hourglass silhouette. Note also the accessories: hat, gloves, umbrella and earrings.

Parkinson's wife Wenda wears British couture label Hardy Amies and strikes a highly stylised pose. To create the right mood when drawing vintage styles – and to capture the right silhouette – it helps to recreate period poses. Look at the croquis on pages 32–35 to see how silhouettes and poses changed. Photographs from the time will also give you a feel of the period.

1960s trouser suit

Draw the V neckline and start with one side of the collar, which has a notched lapel. Continue a line from the base of the collar for the jacket opening.

Add the opposite collar, shoulders and armholes, followed by the body of the jacket. Keep the lines straight to create a boxy shape.

Add simple trousers, tailoring them in slightly at the ankles.

CLOSE-UP
French designer Yves Saint Laurent is famous for his 1960s trouser suits, but it was British design duo Foale and Tuffin (see pages 20–21) who first introduced the trouser suit.

1980s power suit

Start with a soft collar with neat revers, then add wide, oversized shoulders.

Continue lines down from each collar to show the opening of the jacket, then draw the sides of the jacket and the sleeves.

Fill in a short, waisted dress underneath, highlighting a pair of toned, athletic legs.

CLOSE-UP
Wide shoulders and looser tailoring are key to this look. Businesswomen adopted it to make them look tough and efficient, and it became known as 'power dressing'.

Let's draw vintage

Before you begin drawing, you need to learn the basics. This section starts by showing you how to draw a 'croquis', or figure shape, on which you can hang your clothes. It also shows how the croquis changed, to suit the changing tastes of the different decades, from the 1920s to the 1980s and beyond.

You'll also find practical tips on drawing techniques and the effects you can create with different tools and materials.

Once you can draw your croquis with confidence, study the key looks that follow and then dress your croquis in your own interpretation of vintage styles.

Extra information on each look

Do drawings of each vintage look and learn the key features that define it

③

ITIONS

on show?
interest in fashion growing, museums and galleries en to create relevant tions and displays. Find at is happening near you ight prove inspiring.

ual designers
ions are a good way to different vintage periods study specific designers' uch as the following: lexander McQueen Beauty exhibition at the politan Museum in 2011 – had over 650,000 d was one of its most ar shows ever. rienne Westwood tion, organised by the a and Albert Museum 94, has since travelled international venues.

④

ON STAGE

Theatre, ballet and opera
• Going to a play, ballet or opera can inspire ideas for vintage looks. If a production has a period setting, this will have been carefully researched and crafted by a team of people, including the costume designer.
• Study the detail of the costumes, and watch to see how the clothes move when worn.

Period style
• Go to see performances set in the period in which you are interested.
• If you cannot go to a live performance, you can still check out the costumes designed for it. If you are researching 1980s style, for example, find images of the Broadway musical Coco (1969), in which Katharine Hepburn starred as the designer Chanel. The costumes were created by Cecil Beaton, the photographer and Oscar-winning designer.

⑤

SHOPS AND SALES

Vintage shops
• These shops offer a fantastic opportunity to learn about the history of fashion. They allow you to see close-up how clothes were made and to try them on.
• Be careful to distinguish what is truly 'vintage' from second-hand and retro clothing. It is possible to find lots of bad examples of old clothing as well as reproductions of older styles.

Street markets
• Wherever you go in the world, you can find examples of clothing from the past on sale. In some cities there are specialist street markets as well as vintage retailers.
• If you are interested in buying vintage couture, look for labels to distinguish proper couture from designer ready-to-wear. You can always ask the seller about the origins of a garment.

Auction houses
These are another useful place to study clothes, accessories and jewellery at close hand. Items are usually on display before each major sale so that people can see and handle them.

Let's research vintage

The final section of the book will help you learn more about vintage. It gives advice on where to research and get ideas, as well as practical guidance on how to use your sketchbook and collect your ideas on a pinboard, called a 'moodboard'.

You will find some practical advice on how to use your ideas to put together your own collection.

There are also descriptions of a wide range of different fabrics, a list explaining what particular fashion words mean, and an index so you can easily find what you are looking for inside the book.

Fashion timeline 1920s–1950s

Pages 10–13 give you a visual timeline of the key looks and fashion trends of the 20th century. You can find more detail about each decade in the *Let's draw vintage* section on pages 40–83. If you want to know more about designers and styles that appeal to you, look them up in books, magazines and online.

'flapper' dress

sailor-style 'matelot' trousers

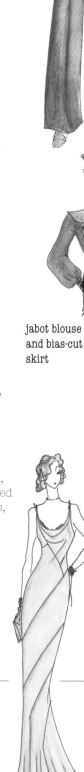

1920s

Key looks
Jazz Age flapper and drop-waisted chemise dresses, knee-length hemlines with fringing and beading, straight-up-and-down silhouette, *garçonne* style, V-shaped necklines, sportswear and bathing suits, Ballets Russes costumes

Key designers
Gabrielle 'Coco' Chanel (1883–1971)
Paul Poiret (1879–1944)
Jeanne Lanvin (1867–1946)
Jean Patou (1880–1936)

Textiles
Jersey, velvet, satin, silk, rayon, embroidered and brocaded fabrics, Modernist prints on devoré textiles

Accessories and trends
Cloche hats, two-tone and T-bar shoes, Cuban and Louis XIV heels, bobbed or cropped hair, designer perfumes, fringed shawls, costume jewellery, suntanned skin

Fashion icons
Adele Astaire, Josephine Baker, Clara Bow, Louise Brooks, Nina Hamnett, Suzanne Lenglen

sporty style

See pages 40–41

cocoon coat

1930s

Key looks
Golden Age of Hollywood, Paris couture, longer hemlines, the siren dress, bolero jackets over backless dresses, halter necks, bias-cut and draped styles, tailored day suits, high-waisted wide trousers

Key designers
Adrian (1903–59)
Madeleine Vionnet (1876–1975)
Elsa Schiaparelli (1890–1973)
Alix 'Madame' Grès (1903–93)
Norman Hartnell (1901–79)
Charles James (1906–78)
Mainbocher (1890–1976)

Textiles
Synthetics, elasticated fabrics, fine wools, tweed, fur, satin, silks, linens, cotton lawn, muslin, organdie, silk crêpe

Accessories and trends
Softly waved hair, zips, shoulder pads, brassières, gloves, Surrealism, small hats worn at an angle, corseted underwear, tortoiseshell sunglasses, platform soles and sandals

Fashion icons
Joan Crawford, Greta Garbo, Marlene Dietrich, Amelia Earhart, Lee Miller, Ginger Rogers, Gertrude Lawrence, Duchess of Windsor Wallis Simpson, Gloria Swanson

jabot blouse and bias-cut skirt

See pages 42–43

bias-cut evening gown

poodle skirt

Utility dress

1940s

Key looks
Shirtwaister dresses, Utility suits and dresses, trench coats, uniforms, overalls, military details, 'make-do-and-mend' home dress-making with rationed materials, nipped-in or belted waists, A-line skirts with kick pleats, knee-length hemlines, American big band dance-hall style

Key designers
Claire McCardell (1905-58) Incorporated Society of London Fashion Designers including Norman Hartnell, Edward Molyneux, Hardy Amies, Digby Morton and Victor Stiebel (from 1942) Chambre Syndicale de la Haute Couture Parisienne (from 1946)

Textiles
Rayon, wool, cotton, patriotic printed textiles

Accessories and trends
Wide-brimmed and pillbox hats, berets, headscarves and turbans, elaborate hairstyles, nylon stockings, cork and wooden wedge soles

Fashion icons
Lauren Bacall, Bette Davis, Rita Hayworth, Celia Johnson, Barbara Stanwyck

'make-do-and-mend' dress

1950s

Key looks
The New Look, tight-waisted boned bodices with full or pencil-slim skirts, the sack dress, unstructured day suits, raglan sleeves, debutante ball gowns, rockabilly prom dresses, rock 'n' roll poodle skirts, stiff petticoats, cropped trousers

Key designers
Gabrielle 'Coco' Chanel (1883-1971) Cristóbal Balenciaga (1895-1972) Christian Dior (1905-57) Jacques Fath (1912-54) Pierre Balmain (1914-82) Hubert de Givenchy (b.1927)

Textiles
Nylon, silk, wool, tweeds, linen, gingham, denim

Accessories and trends
Matching handbags, gloves and shoes, stiletto heels with pointed toes, ballet shoes, penny loafers, conical brassières, neckscarves, short socks, sunglasses, elasticated 'waspie' belts

Fashion icons
Vivien Leigh, Marilyn Monroe, Queen Elizabeth II, Grace Kelly, Audrey Hepburn

Chanel suit

New Look

See pages 44–45

See pages 46–51 and 54–55

Fashion timeline 1960s–1990s

Follow vintage fashion through the later decades of the 20th century, from the mini-skirts of the 1960s to the minimalist elegance and street-style grunge of the 1990s.

peasant dress

PVC
mini-dress

1960s

Key looks
Shift dresses, mini-skirts, hot pants, trouser suits, babydoll dresses with Peter Pan collars, safari suits, Space-Race style, polo-neck sweaters, cropped capri trousers, second-hand clothes and boutiques

Key designers
Emilio Pucci (1914-92)
Pierre Cardin (b.1922)
Mary Quant (b.1934)
André Courrèges (b.1923)
Barbara Hulanicki (b.1936)
Yves Saint Laurent (1936-2008)
Betsey Johnson (b.1942)

Textiles
PVC plastics, Perspex, paper, corduroy, printed cotton, metal, denim, cheese- and terry-cloth, Op Art, Pop Art, Art Nouveau and psychedelic prints

Accessories and trends
Go-go boots, flat shoes, bouffant and geometric haircuts, false eyelashes, brightly coloured tights, big buckles, Indian jewellery

Fashion icons
Brigitte Bardot, *Barbarella*, Julie Christie, Marsha Hunt, Jacqueline Kennedy, Jean Shrimpton, Twiggy

hot pants

See pages 56–59

1970s

Key looks
The maxi-dress, hippy kaftans, Flower Power flares, glam and glitter, conceptual chic, elaborate knitwear, appliqué motifs, disco jumpsuits, the wrap dress, drainpipe trousers, satin baseball jackets, sweater sets, nostalgia for Victorian and Edwardian designs, prairie dresses, folk style, full-length coats with voluminous skirts

Key designers
Ossie Clark (1942-96)
Thea Porter (1927-2000)
Bill Gibb (1943-88)
Zandra Rhodes (b.1940)
Gina Fratini (b.1931)
Laura Ashley (1925-85)

Textiles
Silk jersey, rayon jersey, lurex, lamé, Lycra, silk, tartan, feathers, studs, sequins, metallic leathers, mohair, denim, crêpe

Accessories and trends
Bondage trousers, safety pins, chunky boots, platform shoes

Fashion icons
David Bowie, *Annie Hall*, Mia Farrow, Jerry Hall, Farrah Fawcett, Iman, Lauren Hutton

flared jeans

punk style

See pages 60–65

grunge floral dress

ruffles and
underwear
as outerwear

tomboy style

simple
silhouette

slouchy suit

1980s

Key looks
Power-dressing, Paris *prêt-à-porter*,
body-con (close-fitting) bandage
dresses, pirate frills, baroque
corsets, underwear as outerwear,
deconstruction, Japanese and
Belgian intellectual chic

Key designers
Vivienne Westwood (b.1941)
Issey Miyake (b.1938)
Rei Kawakubo (b.1942)
Donna Karan (b.1948)
Azzedine Alaïa (b.1940)
Christian Lacroix (b.1951)
Jean Paul Gaultier (b.1952)
Dries van Noten (b.1958)

Textiles
Lace, Lycra, silk damask, devoré
velvet, polyester pleating, mohair,
jewelled velvet

Accessories and trends
Leotards, leggings, the filofax,
devoré velvet scarves, gilt buttons,
conical bras, batwing sleeves,
puffball skirts, slogan T-shirts,
plastic bangles

Fashion icons
Cindy Crawford, Linda Evangelista,
Grace Jones, Cyndi Lauper,
Madonna, Molly Ringwald,
Diana, Princess of Wales

See pages 74-77

1990s

Key looks
Minimalism, street-style grunge,
combat trousers, teen-pop overalls,
cheongsam dresses, red-carpet
glamour, supermodels, theatrical
fashion shows

Key designers
Calvin Klein (b.1942)
Jil Sander (b.1943)
Helmut Lang (b.1956)
Gianni Versace (1946-97)
Marc Jacobs (b.1963)
Alexander McQueen (1969-2010)

Textiles
Flannel, denim, eco-friendly
textiles, organic cotton, cashmere,
pure wool, Lycra, leather and
imitation leather, rhinestones

Accessories and trends
Designer logos, status shoes,
sneakers, Dr Martens boots,
tattoos, mobile phones,
pashminas, the Wonderbra,
the It bag, a neutral colour palette

Fashion icons
Courtney Love, Stella Tennant,
Kristen McMenamy,
Kate Moss, Naomi Campbell

See pages 80-83

Trend: **The 1920s flapper dress**
Designers: **Jean Patou and Miuccia Prada**
Signature look: **Straight shift dress**
Key features:

- **Dropped waistlines and loose, clean lines**
- **Hemlines just below the knee**
- **Sheer delicate fabrics with fur trimmings, beaded embellishment and embroidery**

Who loves this look?
Dennis Nothdruft, Curator at the Fashion and Textile Museum, London

Jean Patou

Miuccia Prada

Dennis Nothdruft says ...

'The 1920s is one of the most exciting periods in fashion history. After World War I, designers such as Patou and Chanel responded to the changes in people's lives with new ideas for how they should dress. Many of the styles that are popular today – from jersey tops to women's trousers – were first introduced in the 1920s.

The dropped-waist flapper dress is perhaps the most influential 1920s look. The silhouette remains popular in 21st-century fashion. It was given an alternative contemporary twist in 2013 when leading fashion designer Miuccia Prada was asked to collaborate on the vintage costume design for a film of the F. Scott Fitzgerald book *The Great Gatsby* (1925).'

Who was Jean Patou?

Jean Patou (1880–1936) was a French fashion designer who helped to create what is now considered the 1920s 'look', including the famous flapper dress. Patou led the development of elegant, practical clothing and a long, lean silhouette. To take advantage of the growing market for sportswear in the 1920s, he opened salons in Deauville and Biarritz – two French seaside resorts – where he sold swimsuits and yachting outfits alongside sweater sets. His business expanded in America, too.

It is the Patou brand itself that is his lasting legacy, from the 'JP' monogram to the company's famous perfumes, including the first scent for both men and women, made in 1928.

Who is Miuccia Prada?

Miuccia Prada (born 1949) leads the design house Prada, which was originally a luxury goods firm established in 1913. She is widely regarded as a trendsetter in present-day fashion, and has been a leading name in international fashion for more than 25 years.

Her work is known for being highly original, from the black nylon handbags that she introduced in the 1980s to her costume designs for the 2013 film *The Great Gatsby*, in collaboration with the costume designer Catherine Martin.

Prada's designs often feature clever new combinations of classic silhouettes and materials, to create a cool and luxurious feel.

These designs by Patou show the simple, sporty shapes he developed, which came to embody the 1920s look and the clothes worn by 'flappers'. Flappers were a new breed of young women who rejected the more conservative fashions and conventions of the previous generation.

Actress Carey Mulligan played Daisy Buchanan in the 2013 film *The Great Gatsby*, which was set in the 1920s. This dress was inspired by Prada's beaded chandelier dress from her spring/summer 2010 collection.

Prada made about 20 dresses for each of the ball scenes in *The Great Gatsby*. All were selected from her past collections and restyled slightly to feel more in keeping with the period.

Trend: **Surreal fashion**
Designer: **Elsa Schiaparelli**
Signature look: **Intelligent and playful designs**
Key features:
- **Elegant black dresses**
- **Witty embroidered motifs**
- **Novelty buttons and details**

Who loves this look?
Kerry Taylor, auctioneer of vintage clothes

Elsa Schiaparelli

Kerry Taylor says ...

'Schiap, as she liked to be known (she hated her Christian name) produced clothes that were not just beautiful, but whimsical and interesting. She believed that clothes should be architectural, 'that the body must never be forgotten and it must be used as a frame is used in a building'. Construction was always of prime importance.

Schiap collaborated on some of her major collections with Salvador Dalí, which resulted in hats shaped like telephones and organza dresses printed with lobsters. Her clothes are magical, clever and playful and she is rightly regarded as one of the greatest designers of the 20th century.'

Who was Elsa Schiaparelli?

The Italian designer Schiaparelli (1890–1973) is celebrated for her artistic and witty fashion creations. She wrote that, 'Dress designing is to me not a profession but an art'.

Schiaparelli moved between Rome, New York and Paris in the 1920s, and she was influenced by the art movement Surrealism. Surrealists created weird, dream-like artworks. Schiaparelli collaborated with the artist Salvador Dalí and the writer and film-maker Jean Cocteau, and the results are among the most valuable and desirable pieces of 20th-century haute couture.

Like the Surrealists, Schiaparelli loved to shock. Her best-known perfume was called Shocking and her favourite colour was shocking pink. In the 1930s, she promoted the culottes or 'trouser-skirt' for women.

Schiaparelli was one of the first designers to present themed collections – from the circus to the night sky. She was also the first to open a boutique alongside her couture salon, selling fashion separates, perfume, accessories and costume jewellery.

Details were a key feature of Schiaparelli's designs. She championed the use of zip fasteners in evening wear and prized unusual fabrics, including textured weaves, cloth made from glass, and specially commissioned prints or Highland tweeds. Her clothes often had buttons made of precious metals, moulded leather or other extraordinary materials. Embroidery by Maison Lesage, the specialist Paris couture house, provided the finishing touches to her sumptuous evening capes, jackets and dresses.

Schiaparelli was famed for her avant-garde creations, but she was also a good businesswoman. She included sophisticated black evening gowns in every collection to appeal to a wider clientele.

Two outfits in the style of Schiaparelli. Notice the red lips trimming the pockets on the left-hand outfit.

Embellished with gold thread and star-shaped beads, the jacket also glitters with glass shooting stars, embroidered comet tails and a dusting of tiny glass beads.

Inspired by the night sky and the signs of the zodiac, this midnight-blue velvet jacket was embroidered by Maison Lesage.

Trend: **The 1950s New Look**
Designers: **Christian Dior; taken up by the Incorporated Society of London Fashion Designers and other designers worldwide**
Signature look: **Elegant, fabulously tailored formal gowns**
Key features:
- **Firmly boned bodices and tiny waistlines**
- **Long full-skirted evening dresses**
- **Luxurious use of fabric**

Who loves this look?
Elizabeth Smith, who directs the archive of the famous fashion photographer Norman Parkinson

Christian Dior

Elizabeth Smith says:

'The post-war New Look is the subject of some of my favourite fashion images of all time. Norman Parkinson's photographs for British *Vogue* in the 1950s exude a sense of optimism and joy that was a huge turnaround after the drab utilitarianism of the war years. His ability to capture not only the exquisite craftsmanship of the clothes but also the extraordinary elegance of the women who modelled them is compelling. These fairytale dresses worn by high-profile models and celebrities embody an era of elegance: a time of afternoon teas, cocktail parties, theatre outings and balls, and a different oufit for every occasion.'

What was the New Look?

World War II ended in 1945. After the hardships of the war, Parisian couturier Christian Dior (1905–57) brought out a collection of long, full, pleated skirts, boned bodices and corseted jackets. To some, they seemed radical and shocking. For others, his ultra-feminine silhouettes and old-style ideas of luxury and romance seemed like a return to earlier traditions. After seeing his work in 1947, the editor of *Harper's Bazaar* magazine called it the 'New Look'.

In London, couturiers followed the creative lead of Paris. In 1942, the Incorporated Society of London Fashion Designers was founded to promote the British fashion industry. The original members were Hardy Amies, Norman Hartnell, Edward Molyneux, Digby Morton, Bianca Mosca, Peter Russell and Worth (Elspeth Champcommunal). Later, Victor Stiebel and others also joined the Society.

The Society received a boost when Princess Elizabeth became Queen of the United Kingdom in 1952. With the world's media watching her, she took British fashion design to a truly global stage.

The London Season also resumed after the war, bringing with it a whirl of smart, high-society events. Wealthy women needed whole new wardrobes to wear for the Season, which provided plenty of work for the Society.

A Norman Hartnell gown, photographed by Parkinson in 1951.

Christian Dior's 'Mozart' gown. Parkinson took this photograph for Vogue in May 1950.

Parkinson took this photograph in 1957 for British Vogue. It showcases dresses by members of the Incorporated Society of London Fashion Designers.

Trend: **The 1960s mini-dress**
Designers: **Foale and Tuffin**
Signature look: **D-dress**
Key features:
- **Simple shift dress**
- **D-shaped patch pocket in bold red and yellow**
- **Boxy, graphic shape and colours of pocket echo the Pop Art style of the period**
- **A fresh and new approach to fashion**

Who loves this look?
Sir Paul Smith, designer

Foale and Tuffin

Sir Paul Smith says ...

'Foale and Tuffin were such pioneers. It was so revolutionary what they were doing; it linked the whole pop scene and the worlds of art and graphics. It was just really moving. And they made important work early on. These fantastic girls were really ahead of the game.

Fashion has changed so much these days. Now it's not just about design, but also about marketing. It's about knowing what's going on. Now sadly a lot of it is to do with "following". It's no longer to do with "leading". And I think Sally and Marion actually led. It came from the head and the heart. It wasn't about all the other stuff that we deal with today. So well done them, I say – fantastic.'

Who were Foale and Tuffin?

Marion Foale and Sally Tuffin were two designers who helped to define British fashion in the 1960s. They both trained at Walthamstow Art School and the Royal College of Art, London. They opened a boutique near Carnaby Street in London in 1961.

Foale and Tuffin were praised for the craftsmanship and the detail of their work. They were influenced by celebrated 1960s fashion designer Mary Quant. Their designs paved the way for key trends, such as the shift dress, colourful tights and trouser suits for women.

The famous fashion photographer David Bailey photographed Foale and Tuffin's designs, which appeared regularly in magazines. High-profile women wore their clothes. These included Marit Allen, who edited the 'Young Idea' section of British *Vogue* magazine, and presenter Cathy McGowan on *Ready Steady Go!* – one of the first television programmes to broadcast pop music to a national audience. The famous women who wore the label helped to promote Foale and Tuffin's work to a wide audience.

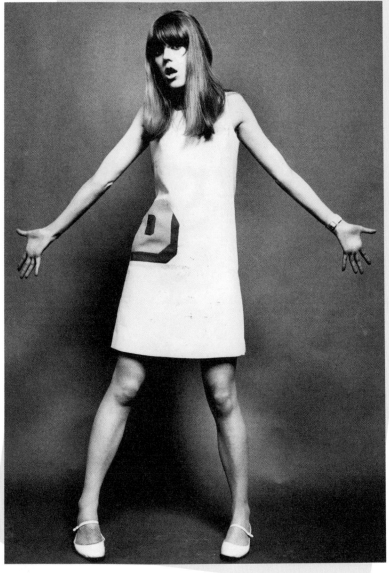

In this drawing by Sally Tuffin, two blocks of different colours emphasise the boxy shapes of the design.

In this photograph, the model Jenny Boyd wears a white linen Double D mini-dress designed by Foale and Tuffin in 1968. The yellow-and-red D-shaped pocket adds a graphic twist to a simple shift dress.

Bold diagonal stripes are used for dramatic effect in this design by Sally Tuffin. An outsized hat completes the look.

Trend: **The 1970s romantic floaty frock**
Designer: **Bill Gibb**
Signature look: **A dress for a fairy-tale princess**
Key features:
- **Long full-skirted gowns with floaty layers**
- **Prints and textiles with embroidery and beadwork**
- **A groundbreaking soft look, contrasting with the clean simple lines of the 1960s**

Who loves this look?
Twiggy, model, actress and singer

Bill Gibb

Twiggy says ...

'It's about time Billy got the recognition he deserves for being a genius. And I think he was a genius.

Bill's talent was enormous. While we were all wearing mini-skirts and angular clothes, he gave us romantic and Renaissance-inspired dresses; pure fantasy clothes in extraordinary fabrics. His dresses made you feel like a princess.

He was unique, ahead of his time, and a forerunner and inspiration for some of the big designers of today. I really do believe Bill Gibb was one of the greatest designers of the 20th century.'

Who was Bill Gibb?

Many believe Bill Gibb (1943–88) was one of the most creative designers of the 20th-century London fashion scene. He trained at the same time as the influential 1960s designers Ossie Clark, Barbara Hulanicki (of the London boutique Biba) and Zandra Rhodes. In 1970, Bill Gibb was crowned Designer of the Year by *Vogue* magazine.

Gibb is remembered for leading the way in the 1970s with fashion inspired by images of fantasy and romance.

His gowns were often based on historical themes, including the idea of the Renaissance princess. His clothes were usually textured with print, pattern, embroidery, beadwork and leather. He loved experimenting with their different combinations.

Gibb had a vivid imagination and great skill at turning designs on paper into clothes for the high-end couture fashion market.

American artist Kaffe Fassett worked with Gibb in a creative partnership. Together they helped to turn knitwear into an art form. Fassett produced brightly coloured prints and patterns, which Gibb used in his designs.

Gibb had a loyal client list that included the screen goddess Elizabeth Taylor and the model Jan de Villeneuve.

Look at the layers of colour, print and fabric in this 1970s design by Gibb. The pattern of the shirt and the skirt repeat gently and both fall in floaty lines.

In 1971, Twiggy starred in the film *The Boy Friend*. She asked Gibb to design outfits for her to wear to the premieres. The dresses were beautifully made and looked like theatrical costumes. These creations brought Gibb further publicity and recognition.

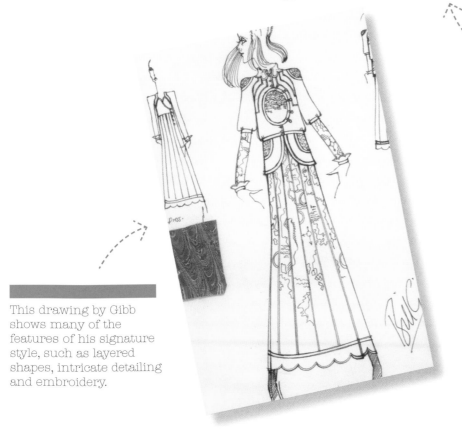

This drawing by Gibb shows many of the features of his signature style, such as layered shapes, intricate detailing and embroidery.

Trend: **Reinventing vintage**
Designer: **Marc Jacobs**
Signature look: **Showgirls on show-stopping catwalks**
Key features:

- **Brazen theatricality, colour and texture**
- **Historical themes with a modern, playful twist**
- **Bold artistic collaborations and sleek accessories**
- **Wide-ranging references, from 19th-century Paris to the East**

Who loves this look?
Kirstin Sinclair, fashion photographer

Marc Jacobs

Kirstin Sinclair says:

'Marc Jacobs is a designer who draws on historical influences to set new directions in fashion. His work incorporates an energising mix of inspirations past and present: whether a reference to a fairground carousel, a department store or a 20th-century motel.

His varied points of reference have allowed him to reinvent the catwalk show as a never-ending arena of inspiration for a photographer. I've been privileged to see numerous beautiful collections come down the runway, but some of the most imaginative shows are those that combine the art of fashion with the emotion of theatre.'

Who is Marc Jacobs?

Marc Jacobs (born 1963) is one of today's most successful global fashion designers. He consistently uses vintage and retro design to create new looks and trends. He is credited with taking grunge and clubwear to the catwalk, and with transforming the fashion house Louis Vuitton.

Born in New York City, Jacobs studied at Parsons School of Design before creating his first Marc Jacobs label collection. In 1987 he received the Council of Fashion Designers of America (CFDA) Perry Ellis Award for New Fashion Talent.

After joining Perry Ellis in 1989, Jacobs created a high-fashion collection inspired by grunge and was chosen as Women's Designer of the Year in 1993 by the CFDA.

Since then Jacobs has designed for his own label, including the youthful line Marc by Marc Jacobs. He has created popular fragrances, eyewear and accessories as well as clothing.

In 1997 Louis Vuitton recruited Jacobs as Artistic Director, and his creative partner Robert Duffy as Studio Director. For 16 years Jacobs and Duffy worked together to bring new flair to the heritage brand.

Their initiatives included collaborations with artists and designers such as Takashi Murakami, Richard Prince and Stephen Sprouse. The sought-after clothing that they created transformed Louis Vuitton's image.

Kate Moss in Marc Jacobs' 2011 autumn/winter collection for Louis Vuitton. The theme of the show was the power of luxury goods, past and present. Vintage styles (including traditional hotel uniforms) mixed with contemporary bags, gloves, belts and boots.

Jessica Stam models a gold velvet bustier with pinstripe trousers in the autumn/winter 2009 Marc Jacobs collection. The combination of businesslike pinstripe trousers and glamorous velvet creates a dramatic and original effect.

Marc Jacobs takes inspiration from history to create something new. These rich colours, sequin embellishments and wide, glittering waspie belts were part of his spring/summer 2011 collection for Louis Vuitton, inspired by Oriental design and 1970s disco.

Try different media

Look at the drawings on these two pages. They all show the same figure but have been drawn with different pencils, pens, paints and ink. Can you see how changing the medium changes the look of the drawing?

Try out different media to discover your favourites. Try combining different media, too.

Look back at the drawings by designers on the previous pages. Do you see how different their styles are? Which media have they used? Which of their styles do you like best? Experiment with using some of their varied techniques to help you develop your own style.

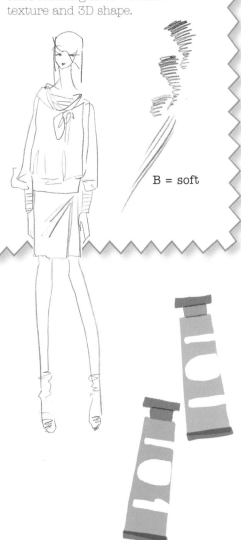

Soft pencil

Use a 4B or softer pencil to create a thick, dark line. Build up your drawing with shading and techniques such as crosshatching – lots of little criss-crossing lines – to add texture and 3D shape.

B = soft

1

H = hard

Hard pencil

This creates a fine line that will highlight the structure and outline of your design. Use a hard pencil when you start drawing to help you focus on shape, outline and the details of how the garment is put together.

Some more ideas

Watercolour is an alternative to gouache paint or felt-tip pen for adding colour to your drawings.
- Watercolour is great for working quickly and adding large areas, or **washes**, of colour.
- Because it is slightly **transparent**, you cannot paint light colours over dark ones.

Brushes are made of various different materials, and the tips come in lots of different shapes and widths. If you are colouring your designs, use a **firm, fine brush** to give you a precise line.

Use a **thin, fine paper** so that you can overlay this on your croquis, or basic figure, and see the shape underneath.
- Watercolour paper may pucker when you apply a wash.

Choose a **sketchbook** that you can carry around easily.

Using an **eraser** can stop you from **learning from your mistakes**. If a design isn't working, you won't find out why by removing the problem. Instead you should draw over it, and find a new line in a different direction. Avoid **rulers**, too – they create hard, mechanical-looking lines.

Pen ③

This versatile medium is good both for outlining and doing detailed drawing. Pens are a great way to give a confident, bold look to your work.

India ink ④

Applied with a brush, India ink gives a soft line. You can use it diluted to fill in areas, too. It's harder to control than other media, but work with your 'mistakes' and follow where they take you.

Gouache ⑤

At some point, you'll need to think about adding colour to your designs. You could use gouache paint, which is a type of watercolour paint. Apply it thickly for solid colour, or thinned-down for a wash.

Where and how to work

Experiment with different **places** for drawing. Working flat – on a table or at a desk, or even on the floor – may be right for you. Or perhaps you could try working on a board at an angle. If it helps to relax you, play music while you draw.

Tracing is useful. Once you have drawn your croquis, or basic figure (see pages 30–35), you can design quickly by drawing over the top of it.
- Place a thin piece of paper over the croquis. Focus on drawing the clothing first. Think about how it sits on the figure.
- When you have completed your design, draw the head, arms, legs and feet, using the croquis as your guide.

Choose the right **line**. A **solid line** indicates a seam and a **broken line** indicates decorative or topstitching.

Small, criss-crossing marks – known as **crosshatching** (see page 28) – help to show areas of light and shade in a design. For example, you could use this technique to show the shadows in the folds of the fabric.

Choosing the right materials

Different prints and fabrics are associated with different vintage looks. Which drawing materials would best convey the textile or texture you want? Here are some ideas to start with.

Faux-fur jacket

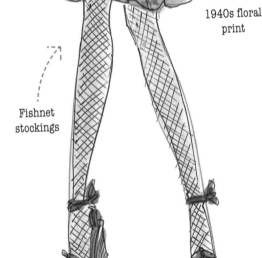

1940s floral print

Fishnet stockings

1940s look

To create a vintage 1940s feel, think about combining traditional materials such as fur, tweed and chiffon with typical floral prints. Give your drawing a modern interpretation by using a contemporary colour scheme such as vibrant orange and sky blue.

Printed textile

Use ink or watercolour to put down a wash of colour as your background. Once this is dry, apply thicker paint in a repeat pattern, such as polka dots or flowers.

Faux-fur

Start with washes of paint, and build up tone to create shadow and depth. Use a fine pen or hard pencil to indicate the long pile of the fur. This should be visible at the edges of the garment.

Fishnet

To create any sort of mesh or net effect, paint in the background in a skin or fabric tone. Using a fine pen or hard pencil, add crosshatching – a network of criss-crossing lines – as evenly and neatly as possible.

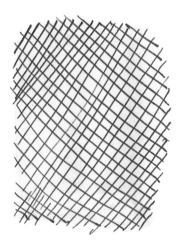

1960s look

Fashion in the later 1960s embraced the mini-skirt silhouette and new synthetic materials such as PVC, used in the tunic here. Metal and plastic accessories were also popular – notice the chunky plastic earrings.

Topstitching

Rib knit

Shiny PVC

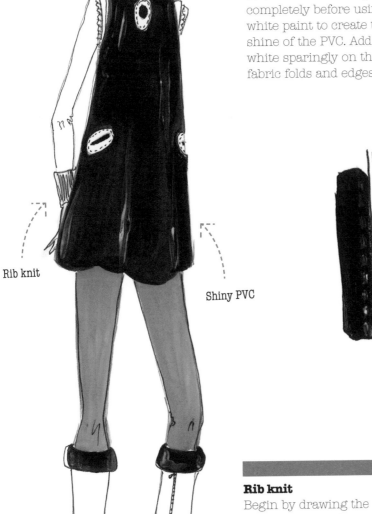

PVC

Put down a thick layer of a strong background colour. Allow it to dry completely before using white paint to create the shine of the PVC. Add white sparingly on the fabric folds and edges.

Topstitching

To create this decorative effect, first identify the seams on your design. Using a fineliner or pen, add a broken line in a contrast colour to indicate topstitching.

Rib knit

Begin by drawing the ribbing on your knitted garment with a pencil. Paint in the bands of colour along the ribbing. When the colour is dry, use a fine pen to further define the ribbed texture.

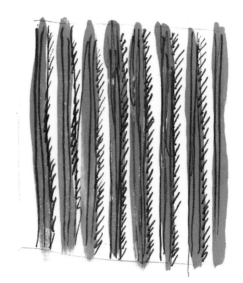

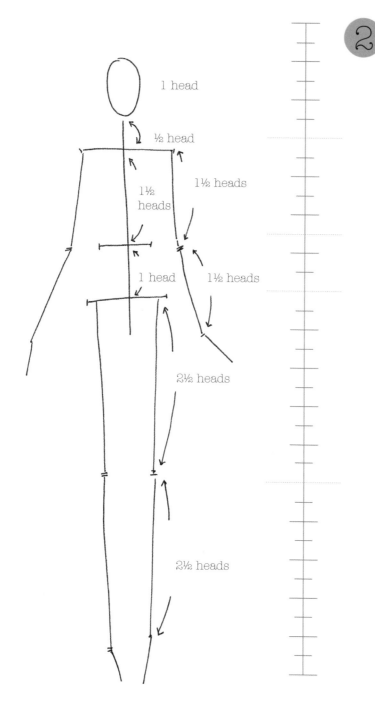

1 head

½ head

1½ heads

1½ heads

1 head

1½ heads

2½ heads

2½ heads

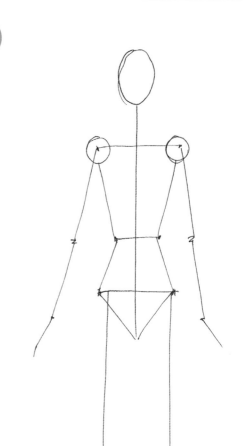

shoulders

waist

hips

knees

Starting with a stick figure

Draw an oval shape for the head. Now draw a line down from it, for the spine. This is the line on which you will 'hang' the rest of the body.

Add three lines for the shoulders, waist and hips. The shoulders are the widest. The waist is about half the width of the shoulders.

Drop down two lines for the legs, starting just inside the hip line. Draw short lines for the feet. Drop down two lines for the upper arms, to the elbows. Draw the lower arms. Add short lines for the hands.

TIP

To check that your drawing is in proportion, measure the height of the head on the page. Place the tip of your pencil on the crown of the head and your thumb at the chin. Use this measurement to check the body's proportions.

Drawing the torso

Draw two circles for the shoulders – imagine each one as a tennis ball. Create a similar shape for each knee.

Starting from each shoulder, draw a line into the waist. From the waist, drop a line to the edge of each hip. You have now created an hourglass shape for the torso – the main part of the body.

From each hip, drop down a further line into the spine to create a triangle. This marks the bottom of the torso.

TIP

Imagine the shoulders as a coat hanger on which you are going to hang your favourite outfit.

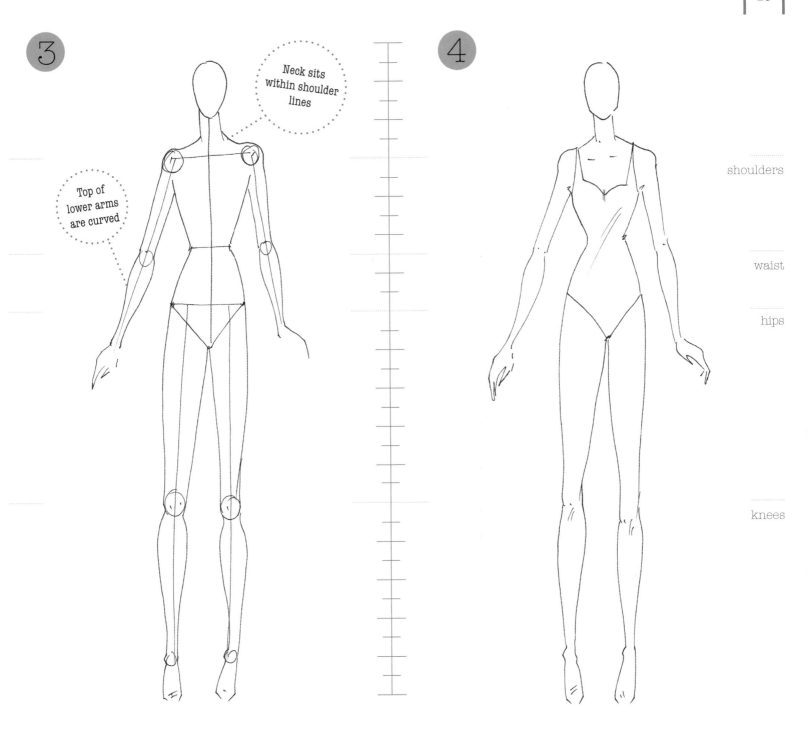

③

④

Neck sits within shoulder lines

Top of lower arms are curved

shoulders

waist

hips

knees

Completing the croquis

For the thighs, draw lines from the outside point of each hip and the bottom of the torso down to the knees.

Draw a small circle for each ankle. For the lower legs, draw curved lines down from the kneecaps to the ankles. Draw the feet.

From the head, drop down two lines for the neck. Draw curved lines for the shoulders.

Add small circles for the elbow joints. Draw lines for the upper arms and forearms, and add the hands.

TIP

Look at your neck in the mirror to check out the shape of your shoulders. When you are drawing the forearms, look at your own forearms to see how they taper towards the wrists.

Creating definition

Now it's time to dress your croquis. Carefully erase your stick figure but keep the outer silhouette you have created. Or you could trace the silhouette (see page 27).

A simple garment to draw is a swimsuit or leotard. Show how the fabric falls across the body by adding movement lines or stress lines, such as creases at the waist.

Adding marks at the joints gives more definition. Add marks to highlight the knees, and make two small marks for the collarbones just below the neck.

TIP

Fashion designers don't always add facial features to their drawings, but you can do so if you wish.

Add hair to suit your design. Pages 36–37 give some examples of hairstyles from different periods.

The changing female shape

A 1989 Bellville Sassoon design for Diana, Princess of Wales

1989

A 1940s Norman Hartnell design for Queen Elizabeth, wife of King George VI

Over the 20th century, changing tastes in fashion emphasised different parts of the female body. So the silhouette looked different in different decades. But the average woman's body shape changed, too. There were social and economic changes, and women's lifestyles and improved diet made a real difference to the female physique. Compare, for example, the typical 1940s silhouette, which has a slim waist and wider shoulders, with the 1980s outline 40 years later. Now, the silhouette has become much sportier, stronger and better defined.

When drawing vintage styles, you will need to adapt your basic croquis or fashion figure template to reflect the style of the era you are featuring. The drawings here and on the following two pages show how the proportions between the bust, waist and hips changed from one decade to the next.

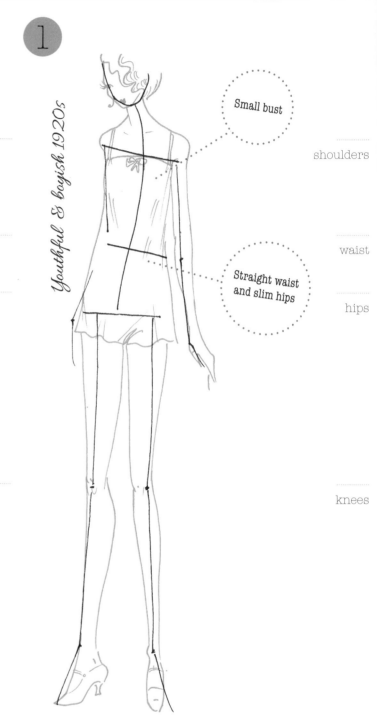

Youthful & boyish 1920s

Small bust

Straight waist and slim hips

shoulders

waist

hips

knees

1920s

For this pose, start with an oval head and straight spine. Add the shoulders, waist and hips, bearing in mind that the fashions of this period did not emphasise the bust or waist.

Drop the lines for each leg straight down from the hips, and mark the knees. Add the joints and draw in shapely calves.

Add marks to emphasise the joints and collarbones.

CLOSE-UP

The fashionable 1920s look was a straight-up-and-down silhouette. Hemlines rose to make a feature of women's legs and ankles, and more women began to wear trousers. Compare the boyish 1920s silhouette with the curvy one from the 1940s.

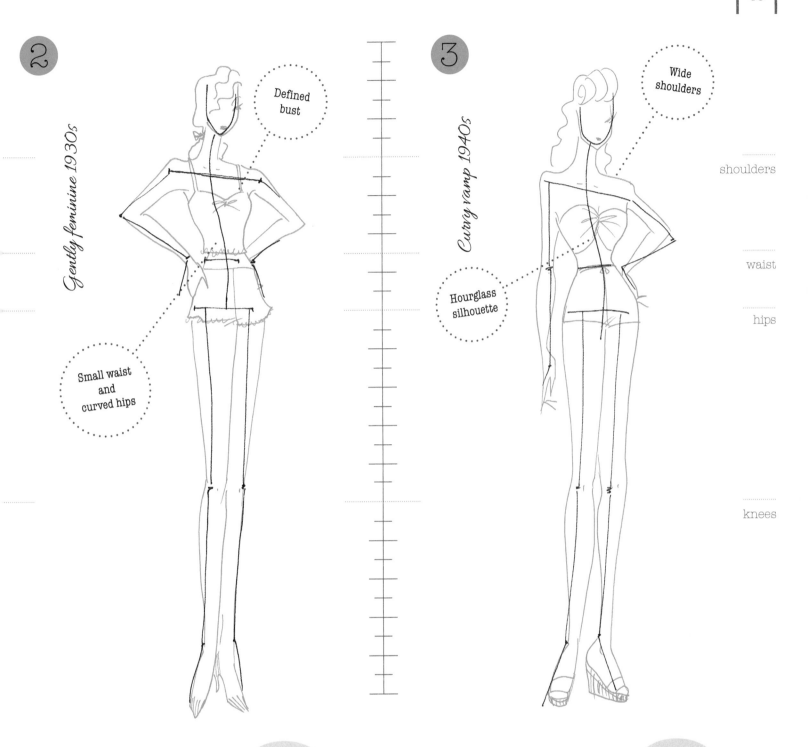

② *Gently feminine 1930s*

Defined bust

Small waist and curved hips

③ *Curvy vamp 1940s*

Wide shoulders

Hourglass silhouette

shoulders

waist

hips

knees

1930s

Draw the head and a straight spine. Focus on the proportions of the shoulders, waist and hips. The waist is about half the width of the shoulders.

From the shoulders, draw the arms straight down or bent with the hands on the hips. Remember arms may be longer than you think.

Draw the long, straight legs. In the 1930s the legs were not on show so much. From 1929 hemlines dropped, and evening gowns remained long throughout the decade.

CLOSE-UP

Note how the 1930s silhouette has changed from the 1920s, with a slender but more defined shape. New kinds of underwear helped women to emphasise the curves they had tried to flatten in the previous decade.

1940s

Draw an oval head and add the spine. Remember the neck is about half the height of the head. Add the shoulders, waist and hips. The shoulders should be the widest point.

From the shoulders, draw the arms. Fill in the torso, emphasising the bust, slim waist and curved hips.

Draw the long, shapely legs. The legs were more on show again. Hemlines during the 1940s usually fell just below the knee.

CLOSE-UP

The typical 1940s figure has wide shoulders with a narrow waist and well-defined bust and hips. Look at photos of female icons of the 1940s, such as the film stars Lana Turner and Rita Hayworth.

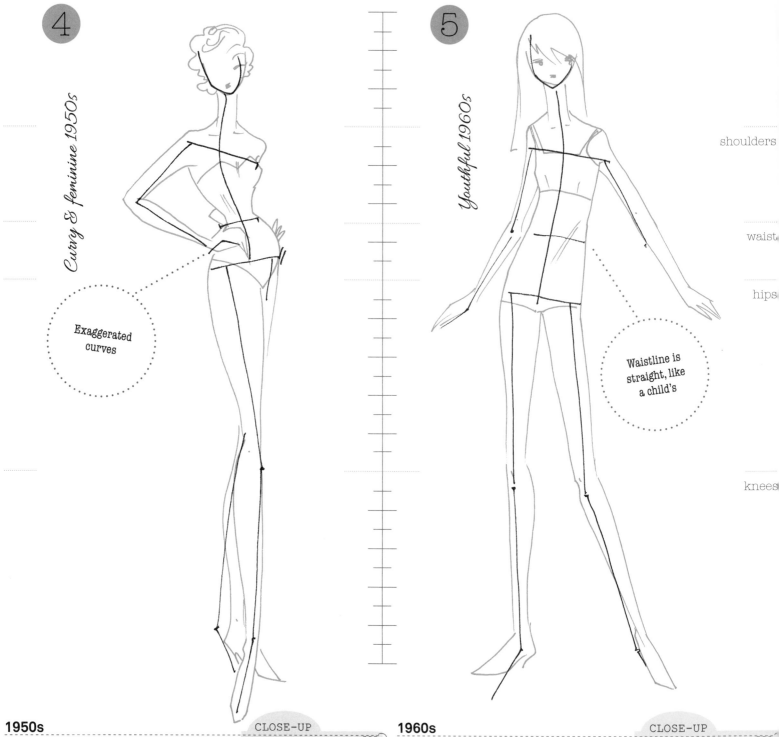

4

Curvy & feminine 1950s

Exaggerated curves

5

Youthful 1960s

Waistline is straight, like a child's

shoulders

waist

hips

knees

1950s

Draw an oval head, then stretch the neck and exaggerate the curve of the spine in a gentle S shape. Add a narrow waistline, and wider lines drawn at angles across the spine for the hips and shoulders.

Drop a line from the raised hip to the foot for the straight rear leg. Mark the knee and ankle. Drop a line for the front leg, from the lower hip inwards to the knee, then a line out to the ankle.

From the highest shoulder draw the arm bent out at the elbow with the hand resting near the hip. Fill in defined thighs and slim calves.

CLOSE-UP

Fashion in the 1950s was tailored to an hourglass silhouette, with tiny waists and exaggerated hips and busts. Models were often photographed in highly stylised poses. Look at the photograph of Wenda Parkinson on page 53.

1960s

For this pose, start with a gently curving spine. Draw the shoulders, waist and hips at a slight angle. Keep the width of these similar and lengthen the torso to emphasise a younger, boyish frame.

Drop a straight line for the left leg from the higher hip, marking the knee. Drop a line straight down to the right knee. Remember to measure two-and-a-half heads below each hip when marking the knee.

Bend the line out to the ankle joint, just wide of the shoulder.

CLOSE-UP

Compare the 1960s silhouette with the curvy 1950s one. Younger models such as Twiggy became very famous and promoted a youthful, almost childlike look. This suited the mini-dress and other fashions of the period.

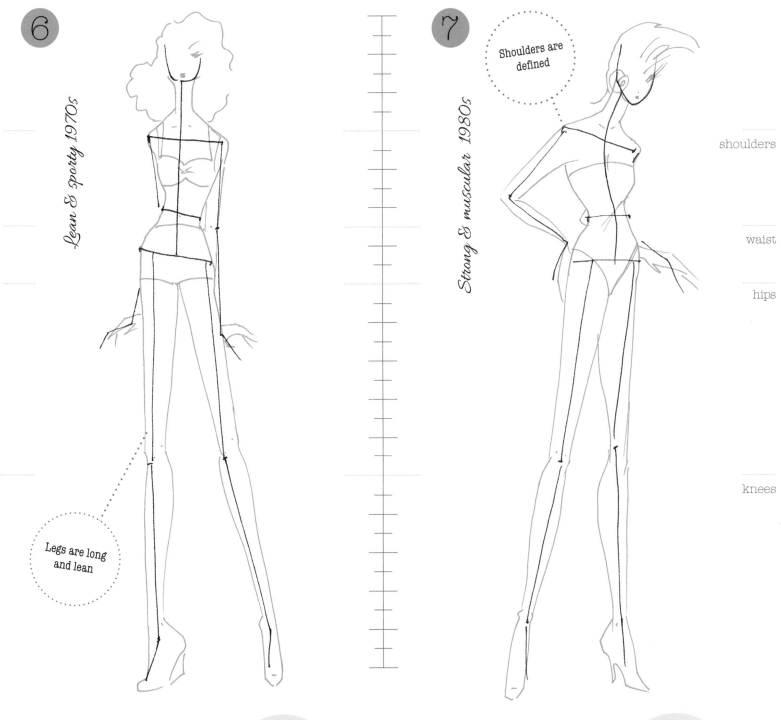

6 *Lean & sporty 1970s*

Legs are long and lean

7 *Strong & muscular 1980s*

Shoulders are defined

shoulders

waist

hips

knees

1970s

Draw a straight line down from the head, adding lines for the shoulders and waist at slight angles.

Drop two lines for the legs, bending the right leg slightly at the knee.

From the right shoulder, draw a smooth line to below the waist and mark the elbow. Continue the same distance again for the forearm. Add the left arm behind the torso.

Draw tiny circles to mark the joints. Fill in the silhouette, emphasising the lean shape of the arms and legs.

CLOSE-UP

In the 1970s, fashion designs took on a very lean and sporty silhouette. Look at photos of 1970s models such as Jerry Hall. What poses do 1970s models strike?

1980s

Draw a softer S curve for the spine, emphasising wide shoulders. Add lines for the waist and hips in closer proportion to each other.

Note the angle of the shoulders with this pose, and the hand positioned on the hips. All the movement in the figure is in the upper part of the body. Legs should be drawn straight down from the hips.

CLOSE-UP

In the 1980s a group of women, including Linda Evangelista and Cindy Crawford, came to be known as 'supermodels'. This was not only because of the money and fame they had, but also because they had strong, 'super' silhouettes.

Proportions of the head

Adding a period hairstyle to your croquis will help to complete the vintage look. Here are some 20th-century hairstyles to choose from. Remember that it's important to get the proportions of the face and head right, too.

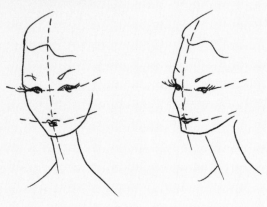

Start with an oval shape for the head and imagine a horizontal and vertical line crossing directly through the centre. Imagine another horizontal line dividing the lower face. Use these guidelines to position the eyes, nose and lips.

1920s bob and Eton crop

Use a sharp pencil to get a crisp line. Think of the hair as solid – like a helmet on the head. Start with the outline shape and draw this around the head. The hairline usually begins a quarter-way down the head.

1

bob

Eton crop

Look at: Louise Brooks and Josephine Baker

1950s waves and pageboy

For the wavy style, start with the hair at the forehead, rising up and curling over. Continue this shape around the face and copy the waves at the back of the head. Begin the pageboy bob with the fringe. Add length and curl underneath.

4

waves

pageboy

Look at: Marilyn Monroe and Audrey Hepburn

5

long, loose hair

geometric cut

Look at: Brigitte Bardot and Mary Quant

1960s geometric and long

Follow the shape of the head for the long hair, then let it hang loosely down around the neck. For the geometric cut, draw a smooth curve around the face and head. Add detail at the ends where the hair strands separate. Create the sharp geometric outline of the bob, pointing it in sharply towards the chin.

②

Marcel waves

chignon

Look at: Marlene Dietrich and the Duchess of Windsor

1930s chignon and Marcel waves

The chignon has a high hairline and round bun shape at the nape of the neck. Add a few lines to show the direction of the hair. For waved hair, start with the outline. Curve the hair around the top of the head and across the face. Fill in the waves inside the outline.

CLOSE-UP

Tight Marcel waves were created with the help of curling irons invented by François Marcel and with new perm technology.

1940s rolls, curls and up-dos

For the Victory Roll, draw the hair curling up over two imaginary rollers above the forehead. Create the outline of the style and suggest how the hair falls. For the up-do, draw the curls high above the head with lines to show the hair pulled back at the sides.

CLOSE-UP

Shoulder-length hair was styled with perms and rollers. The Victory Roll was named to celebrate victory in World War II.

③

Victory Roll

up-do with curls

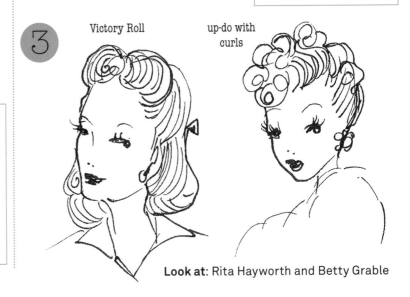

Look at: Rita Hayworth and Betty Grable

1970s curls and feathers

Use a tight wavy line for the curly hair silhouette. Add a mass of curls around the face and head. For the feathered style, draw the parting at an angle. Create the outline curving around the crown of the head and flicking out at the ends and away from the face.

CLOSE-UP

Naturally styled hair was popular in the 1970s. But some looks required tongs and blow-drying. Look at the 1970s TV series *Charlie's Angels*.

⑥

curls

feathers

Look at: Actresses Pam Grier and Farrah Fawcett

⑦

spiky

high-volume

Look at: 1980s Madonna

1980s spiky and high-volume

For the spiky crop, practise drawing the sharp jagged lines that create the silhouette, adding few other features. For the high-volume style, start with the outline shape of the high fringe. Continue the long cascading curls to the shoulders. Fill in the detail.

CLOSE-UP

High-volume scrunched curls and spiky hair defined the 1980s – thanks to hair mousse and gels. Check out Madonna in the film *Desperately Seeking Susan* (1985).

Heel shapes

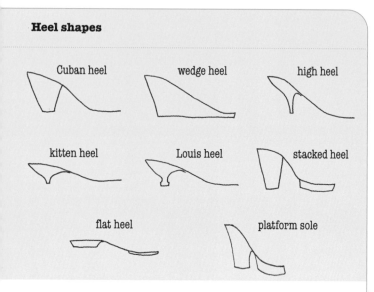

Cuban heel   wedge heel   high heel

kitten heel   Louis heel   stacked heel

flat heel   platform sole

The three main parts of a shoe are the upper that forms the whole top, the sole that runs all the way under the shoe, and the heel.

Different-shaped heels were popular at different times and gave each shoe its own distinctive style. Have a look at the heels above and see where they appear on these two pages.

small, double-handled bag

T-bar shoes

Louis heels

1920s bar shoes and t-straps

A shoe comprises a sole, heel and upper. Start with the shape of the sole, which supports the foot. Fill in the upper, curving around the heel, cutting away to reveal the foot. Add straps or laces with piping and appliqué details.

CLOSE-UP

Shoes became more visible as skirt lengths rose after World War I. Straps helped to keep shoes on while dancing.

1950s stilettos and ankle-straps

For the stiletto, visualise the slim outline of the heel and draw the angle of the sole with this in mind. Draw one of the variety of uppers that were popular, from filled-in court shoes to open-toe marabou mules. Attach ankle straps at the heel.

CLOSE-UP

In the 1950s, Charles Jourdan and Roger Vivier created sharp stiletto designs for sophisticated wear. Metal cores made the thin stiletto heels strong.

marabou mule

wristlet bag

ankle strap

court shoe with stiletto heel

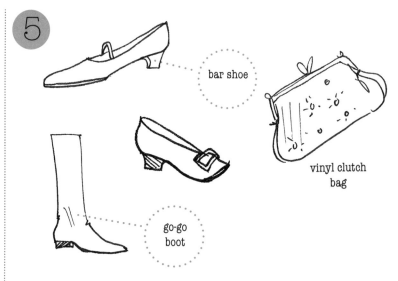

bar shoe

vinyl clutch bag

go-go boot

1960s go-go boots and low heels

For the low-heeled bar shoe, draw a gently sloped sole and neat heel. Fill in the upper with a low, wide opening for the foot. Add a square heel and buckle for a different look. For the go-go boot, keep the upper tight around the ankle and calf.

CLOSE-UP

The 1960s saw mini-skirts worn with calf-high or knee-high vinyl boots, or low-heeled shoes with buckles or straps.

1930s heeled pumps and sports shoes

Start with the line of the sole. Think about the height and shape of the heel, from flat brogues to high evening shoes. Create an elegant outline for the upper that reveals the bridge of the foot and has a rounded toe.

CLOSE-UP

Styles evolved in the 1930s for women's work, sports, daywear and evening wear. They ranged from lace-ups to high-heeled pump shoes for evening.

1940s stacked heels and Utility shoes

Think about the angle of the foot: whether it is seen straight or side-on. Start the sole of the wedge sandals with a flat line. Add the upwards curve of the platform. Select between a closed or open toe and heel, then fill in the upper.

CLOSE-UP

Materials for making shoes were in short supply during World War II. Cork soles and other substitutes were used instead. For more about Utility wear, see page 44.

1970s platform soles and sandals

For platforms, draw the angled sole first and add the platform and heel beneath. Add the upper with wide sandal straps, or a more conservative court style. Use details to suggest materials such as metallic leathers or bonded wood soles.

CLOSE-UP

The 1970s featured platform soles in metallic leathers and bold colours. Try flat wide heels, clogs and strappy disco sandals with your 1970s-inspired designs, too.

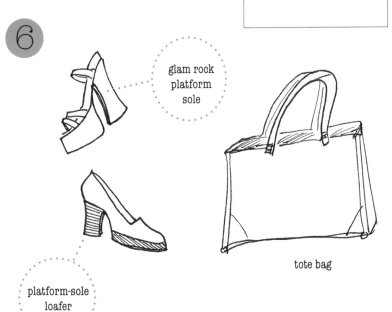

1980s ankle boots and mules

For the granny boot and court shoe, draw a sharp angle above the heel. Add a creased outline and a wide horizontal opening for the scrunch boot. Note the granny boot details and the gentler sole and open back of the mule.

CLOSE-UP

In the 1980s power suits worn with court shoes and glamorous mules contrasted with street-style 'scrunch' and 'granny' boots.

1

all that jazz

Chiffon was popular

2

Coat hangs straight down from shoulders

shoulders

waist

hips

knees

Flapper dress

Draw a deep V shape, starting in the middle of each shoulder and meeting below the bustline. Add low armholes and draw the tunic following the shape of the body.

Below the waistline, add a wide sash gathered in a rose shape.

Drop two lines for the skirt and create a scalloped 'lettuce-edge' hemline. Add stress lines below the sash to suggest a lightweight, delicate fabric.

CLOSE-UP

Fashion in the 1920s was designed to allow free movement. This made it easy to dance to the new popular music – jazz. Notice how all the designs on these two pages follow the same basic silhouette.

Velvet cocoon coat

Start with a low V-shaped neckline. Add a soft collar, rising up behind the neck, curving around the shoulders and then narrowing to meet at the base of the V.

Draw the centre fastening, and then drop a line curving out to one knee for the opening.

Add the sides of the coat and loose sleeves, using curved lines to create volume. Show the hemline of the dress where the coat parts.

CLOSE-UP

Imagine the collar is fluffy like a pillow. Padding and quilting were used in the 1920s to add comfort and luxury to garments.

3

Long sweater conceals body curves

anyone for tennis?

cloche hats

beret

Louis XIV heel

brogue

loafer

ankle-strap shoe

handbags

Sportswear ensemble

Draw the sweater first, with a wide V-shaped neckline and narrow shoulders. Drop two lines from the shoulder to the hipline to create a long, straight body. Then add the narrow sleeves.

Just inside the hem of the sweater, drop two lines for the skirt silhouette. Add the pleats, joining these at different heights at the hemline.

Use short straight lines to indicate the ribbed hems of the sweater, and draw in a scarf.

CLOSE-UP

This was a typical outfit to wear when playing golf or perhaps tennis. In the first half of the 20th century, 'sportswear' was usually worn to watch sport rather than to play it.

In the 1920s, young women rebelled against tradition. They cut their hair into short bobs, wore shorter skirts and listened to a new kind of music called jazz. They were called 'flappers' and the decade was dubbed the Jazz Age. Twenties designs feature a boyish shape that hides feminine curves. The loosely fitting designs reflect the new freedoms of the age.

Typical 1920s accessories include shoes with ankle straps or T-bars and Louis XIV heels, pretty bags with fringing, and berets and cloche hats. The term 'cloche' derives from the French word for bell, and these hats fitted closely around the head, echoing the neat, short, boyish hairstyles of the period.

Mermaid dress

Draw the straight neckline and decorative ruffled sleeves. Follow the curved outline of the body to the knees and draw two long darts under the bust along the ribcage.

Join up the hem with a small corsage (bunch of flowers). Flare out the mermaid skirt, using lines to show the fullness of the fabric.

CLOSE-UP

This silhouette is like a mermaid's tail – closely fitting to the knees, then flaring out. This design is inspired by a dress worn by actress Joan Crawford in the film *Letty Lynton* (1932).

Jabot blouse and bias-cut skirt

Start with a V-shaped neckline. Add a sailor-style collar that gathers into a jabot, or ruffle. Create the loose wide sleeves, gathering them into each cuff. Draw the sides of the blouse into a high, tight waistband.

Add the outline of the skirt, following the hips. Flare the skirt below the knees and join up the hem.

CLOSE-UP

This long, lean silhouette is typical of the 1930s. The jabot is the decorative ruffle at the neck. A simple but sophisticated skirt balances the frilly blouse.

Ruffles emphasise shoulders

Figure-hugging silhouette

Skirt flares at knee

Small waist

Wide collar and frills

Figure-hugging skirt

Mid-calf hemline

shoulders

waist

hips

knees

'Matelot' trousers

Draw the high turtleneck. Add the shoulders and the sleeves, then fill in the sides of the sweater.

Curve the waistband upwards into the centre. Draw the outer line of the trousers closely around the hips, then straight down wide of the body for the legs. Add straight centre pleats, and button pocket fastenings.

CLOSE-UP

Matelot is French for 'sailor'. The fitted waistband of these sailor-style trousers emphasises the waist, which was a focal point in 1930s fashion.

Town and country suit

For the neckline, draw a curvy V-shape, shading in the blouse beneath. Add the wide, soft collar. From the base of the V continue the line down across the right lapel to become the jacket opening.

Draw the shoulders, arms and sides of the jacket, emphasising the waist with a belt. Continue the skirt down to the calves. Join up the hem.

CLOSE-UP

Hemlines dropped during the 1930s. They varied according to the type of clothing. Evening dresses were usually full length, afternoon wear was low-calf and daywear was mid-calf.

all aboard!

Small waist

Wide legs make waist look smaller

Wide lapels

Fitted jacket

Neatly fitting skirt

Mid-calf hemline

shoulders

waist

hips

knees

What's in the look?

The Cotswold Country: Model in dress by Norman Hartnell, Vogue, 1942
Photograph by Norman Parkinson

During World War II, which lasted from 1939 to 1945, fabric was rationed. People were allowed to use only fixed quantities. In Britain, the Board of Trade tried to help by introducing 'Utility' designs that needed less fabric and could be put together easily.

Women's clothing at this time included uniforms and work overalls. Women wore trousers for certain jobs but the day dress was the most common outfit for leisure wear. The key features of a Utility day dress are: a simple silhouette that needs little fabric, a neat collar and sleeves, a belted waist and a knee-length skirt. This dress was worn with practical shoes. To keep their hair tidy, working women often wore a headscarf or turban.

In this 1942 photograph by Norman Parkinson for British Vogue, the model wears a day dress designed by Norman Hartnell as part of the 1941 Utility Clothing scheme.

1

Neat, high collar

Tie belt emphasises waistline

Flared skirt

shoulders

waist

hips

knees

Utility dress

Draw a round neckline followed by the sides and curved edges of the collar. Drop a line down the centre of the blouse for the opening.

Add the loose, short puffed sleeves, detailing the bow at each cuff. Gather the sides of the blouse into a tied waist.

Draw the skirt silhouette, flaring out towards the knee. Add the centre pleat and join up the hem. Detail the pockets. Use lines to show how the fabric gathers in at the waist.

CLOSE-UP

During World War II, printed fabrics were sometimes used to add colour and variety to clothes. What textile patterns would you choose for the dresses on this spread?

②

Short puffed sleeves

High, slim waistline

Skirt ends at knee

waste not want not

③

High neckline

Elaborate hairstyle

Bodice follows shape of body

Softly pleated skirt

shoulders

waist

hips

knees

Make-do-and-mend dress

Draw the tight keyhole neckline with a narrow opening. Add the shoulders and armholes, then add the high puffed sleeves.

Continue the armholes down around the body into a high curved waistband below the bust.

Draw the outline of the skirt to follow the shape of the hips. Add a slight flare at the hem and join this up to show how the fabric falls. Add two short darts down from the high waistband.

CLOSE-UP

In wartime, people were encouraged to 'make do and mend' and adapt existing clothes. This dress still has its old high waistline and puffed short sleeves from the 1930s, but it has been shortened to a 1940s length.

Formal day dress

Draw the curved high neckline. Fill in the shoulders, adding a scalloped edge at each sleeve.

Draw the edges of the dress curving in at the waist, over the hips and flaring towards the hem.

Detail the pleats at the neckline and at each sleeve, and the box pleats hanging from each hip.

CLOSE-UP

Buttons and fabric trimmings were controlled during wartime, but detail has been added to this dress with tucks and pleats. Hats were not rationed, so women could use them to dress up an outfit.

Cocktail dress

Draw the fold of fabric – or shelf bust – at the top of the bodice. Use curved lines starting under the arms, with a diagonal across the body to show where the fabric on the bodice meets and is pulled tight.

Fill in the edges of the bodice to emphasise the bust and tight waist, using stress lines at the waist.

Add a full skirt curving out over each hip and away from the body. Add three or four folds of fabric at the hemline.

CLOSE-UP

During the 1950s, wealthy women required lots of outfits for formal social occasions, such as afternoon teas and cocktail parties.

Party dress

Think of this dress in two parts. The tight bodice follows the typical 1950s silhouette emphasising the bust and waist, and the skirt is full.

Start with a heart-shaped neckline, with curved pieces of fabric creating a petal-like effect on the bodice and a peplum at the hips. A peplum is an overskirt or ruffle at the waistline.

Sketch in a series of lines from under the bodice, opening them out into a full skirt shape. Join up the hem.

CLOSE-UP

Crinolines were worn underneath skirts to create volume. Underwear helped to define the fashionable hourglass-shaped silhouette. The new underwear used fabrics that were synthetic, which means man-made.

1

Tightly cinched-in waist

glamour girl

2

Bodice cut from scallop shapes

Peplum at waist

shoulders

waist

hips

knees

Debutante ball gown

Create a strapless neckline above the bust. Draw the bow shape and add folds where the fabric gathers into the knot.

Outline the skirt in a wide arc to show width and volume. Add two pleats at the centre of the skirt and join up the hem to show movement.

CLOSE-UP

In 1950s Britain, wealthy young women made their entry, or debut, into society at the age of eighteen. They were called debutantes and they wore lovely gowns to attend their special 'coming out' balls.

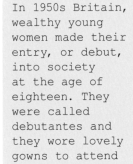

3

party all night!

What's in the look?

London Spring Collections, Hardy Amies strapless ball gown
Vogue, March 1953. Photograph by Norman Parkinson

World War II ended in 1945. After the hardships of the war, Paris became the fashion capital of the world. In 1947, one famous collection defined the style of the coming 1950s. It was created by Paris couturier Christian Dior and it came to be known as the 'New Look'.

The New Look featured elegant jackets and bodices with narrow shoulders, a defined bust and a tiny waist, as well as full, tailored dresses and multi-layered skirts.

Many talented Parisian couturiers followed Dior and created designs that dominated the period. The French shapes and ideas were copied everywhere, and could be seen in films, magazines and on the street.

The couturiers Norman Hartnell and Hardy Amies, among others, introduced the New Look to Britain. The dress above was featured in British *Vogue* in 1953 as part of a feature promoting the work of London designers ahead of the coronation of Queen Elizabeth II.

1 Full skirt

teen princess

2 Tiny waist

rock around the clock

shoulders

waist

hips

knees

Short socks

Prom dress

Create the Y-shaped crossover neckline. Fill in the bodice, with fabric pulled in loosely from either shoulder into the tight waistband.

Draw a very full skirt with wide pleats of fabric, then add the hemline.

CLOSE-UP

Full-skirted gowns were a popular style at high school proms in the 1950s.

Poodle skirt

Starting with the collar, draw in a keyhole opening. Add the shoulders and a soft outline for the sleeves, which gather into a cuff halfway above the elbows.

Create the outline of the blouse and a wide belt. Use stress lines under the bust and above the belt to show how the fabric cinches in.

Draw the skirt flaring out below the belt. Add lines to show the wide folds in the fabric created by the tight belt.

CLOSE-UP

The term 'poodle skirt' comes from the rock 'n' roll era of the 1950s. Wide, swing skirts with fun motifs, such as poodles or musical notes, were popular for dancing. Add your own appliqué motif. How will the folds of fabric affect what can be seen?

3

Tailored
halter top

Rocker dress

Draw one side of the wide collar and drop a short line down the centre of the body to the waist. Complete the other side of the collar, with a line curving under the arm. Then add the sides of the top, following the bustline and waist.

Add a full skirt flaring out wide of the hips. Join up the hem just above the knees with a soft, curving line.

CLOSE-UP

Do you see how this design is a stylised interpretation of 1950s fashion? The dress is slightly shorter but it incorporates a full rock 'n' roll skirt and has a tight, tailored top.

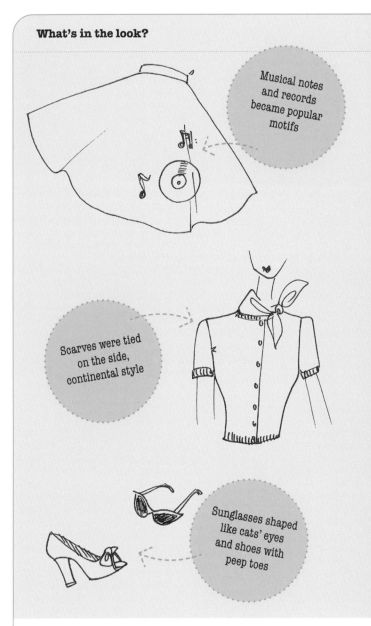

What's in the look?

Musical notes and records became popular motifs

Scarves were tied on the side, continental style

Sunglasses shaped like cats' eyes and shoes with peep toes

Music and fashion often connect to changes in society. By the 1950s, several years after the end of World War II, people felt a new confidence and started spending money more freely.

The 1950s also gave rise to two new inventions: the idea of the 'teenager' as a separate age group and the arrival of rock 'n' roll music.

Rockabilly style is connected to rock 'n' roll and to fashions popular with 1950s teenagers, particularly in America. Cropped capri pants, leather jackets and wide poodle skirts were popular. To make the skirts even fuller, girls wore stiff net petticoats underneath them. Scarves, sunglasses, short socks and shoes completed the look.

What's in the look?

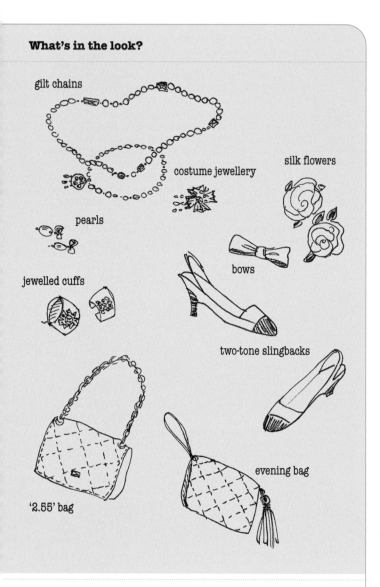

gilt chains

costume jewellery

silk flowers

pearls

jewelled cuffs

bows

two-tone slingbacks

evening bag

'2.55' bag

Collarless neckline

shoulders

Decorative edging

waist

hips

Tweed or bouclé fabric

knees

chic & classy

Accessories are important to the 'Coco Chanel' look. Key elements include long strands of pearls, bold costume jewellery, gilt buttons, two-tone shoes, leather quilted bags and a colour palette of navy, black and cream. Hats are important, too – indeed Chanel's career began when she opened a hat shop in 1909.

Some key pieces even have names. The classic Chanel handbag with its intertwined CC logo and chain strap is known as the '2.55' because it was launched in February 1955.

Research images of Chanel to see how she dressed and styled her own clothes. Many of her most successful designs owed much to her personal taste.

The signature suit

CLOSE-UP

Consider the short, square shape of this jacket and the straight skirt.

Draw the neckline and shoulders first, then the armholes and sides of the top. Use short stress lines beneath the armholes. Continue the neckline down for the jacket opening. Add a trim detail around the neckline, and to mark the pockets.

Draw the loose pencil skirt. Add buttons and a string of pearls.

When Gabrielle 'Coco' Chanel reopened her salon after World War II, her knee-length day suits got a mixed response. But today these signature Chanel suits, in tweed or bouclé fabric, are considered fashion classics.

2

Loose blouse with bow

Soft, loosely fitted jacket

Skirt finishes at mid-calf

3

easy to wear

shoulders

Soft, unfitted jacket

waist

hips

Bow detail

Loose, pyjama-style trousers

knees

1954 collection suit

Use curved lines to create the neck bow of the blouse, then add the lapels and shoulders of the jacket.

Fill in the sides, arms and centre opening of the jacket. The narrow waistband of the skirt sits underneath the jacket. Draw a few lines to show how the blouse tucks in.

Create the narrow silhouette of the skirt. Join up the hem below the knee.

CLOSE-UP

This suit reflects Chanel's values: modern, unstructured and comfortable. In the 1950s Chanel reacted against Christian Dior's formal, corseted 'New Look' (see pages 46–47).

Casual chic trousers

Start with a neat Peter Pan collar and brooch. Add the shoulders, armholes and arms of the jacket. Then draw the turned-back cuff at the end of each sleeve.

Add the front lapels of the jacket and draw the waistband of the trousers with a bow tied at one side.

Follow the outline of your croquis around the hips and continue the line to create the loose trouser legs.

CLOSE-UP

Chanel championed trousers for women, creating soft pyjama-style suits for day and evening wear. The 'Peter Pan' collar was named after the costume worn by actress Maude Adams, who played Peter Pan in 1905.

Crisply shaped jacket

break the mould!

Masculine-style wide legs

Turned-up cuffs

shoulders

waist

hips

knees

1930s masculine suit

Start with the collar, which has a notched lapel. Draw this in two parts. Drop a line down from the lapel on the left to become the jacket opening, flaring out in a cutaway shape.

Draw the shoulders and armholes, then the body of the jacket. Add the sleeves and button details.

Create a high-waisted, wide-legged trouser shape by drawing down the outline of each leg and adding fullness at the hem. Add a centre pleat and cuffs to the trousers.

CLOSE-UP

In the 1930s, it was rare for women to wear the kinds of tailored suits that men wore. Look at photos of film star Marlene Dietrich, who defied convention by adopting masculine-style clothes.

1960s trouser suit

Draw the V neckline and start with one side of the collar, which has a notched lapel. Continue a line from the base of the collar for the jacket opening.

Add the opposite collar, shoulders and armholes, followed by the body of the jacket. Keep the lines straight to create a boxy shape.

Add simple trousers, tailoring them in slightly at the ankles.

CLOSE-UP

French designer Yves Saint Laurent is famous for his 1960s trouser suits, but it was British design duo Foale and Tuffin (see pages 20–21) who first introduced the trouser suit.

③

Wide, padded shoulders

Jacket worn open

power dresser

1980s power suit

Start with a soft collar with neat revers, then add wide, oversized shoulders.

Continue lines down from each collar to show the opening of the jacket, then draw the sides of the jacket and the sleeves.

Fill in a short, waisted dress underneath, highlighting a pair of toned, athletic legs.

CLOSE-UP

Wide shoulders and looser tailoring are key to this look. Businesswomen adopted it to make them look tough and efficient, and it became known as 'power dressing'.

What's in the look?

Hyde Park Corner, Wenda Parkinson in a Hardy Amies suit, Vogue, 1951
Photograph by Norman Parkinson

This photograph by Norman Parkinson shows off 1950s tailoring. Key features of the style include oversized lapels, big pockets and large buttons. The shape of the jacket emphasises the hourglass silhouette. Note also the accessories: hat, gloves, umbrella and earrings.

In the photograph, Parkinson's wife Wenda wears British couture label Hardy Amies and strikes a highly stylised pose. To create the right mood when drawing vintage styles – and to capture the right silhouette – it helps to recreate period poses. Look at the croquis on pages 32–35 to see how silhouettes and poses changed over the decades. Photographs from the time will also give you a feel of the period.

Classic sack dress

Draw a straight line from one shoulder to the other, with a small bow at one side. Drop a line from each shoulder for the armhole, and continue this down to create both sides of the dress.

Add a wide band at the hem, narrowing into a bow. Draw the straight sleeves and add a few stress lines below the bust to suggest the shape.

CLOSE-UP

The sack dress is associated with Spanish fashion designer Cristóbal Balenciaga. In the 1950s, he explored ways to broaden the silhouette at the shoulders to allow clothes to hang freely from the neckline.

Tunic sack dress

Draw a line from the middle of one shoulder to the other. Create the crescent-shaped collar with a tie detail. Draw the straight armholes and three-quarter-length sleeves.

Continue the line of the armholes straight down to the thighs. Draw the hem, with a narrow skirt beneath. Add stress lines where the fabric pulls across the body.

CLOSE-UP

Compare this loose-fitting style with the more formal 1950s New Look (pages 46–47). In the sack dress, the focus is on the simple unfitted shape, with little detail.

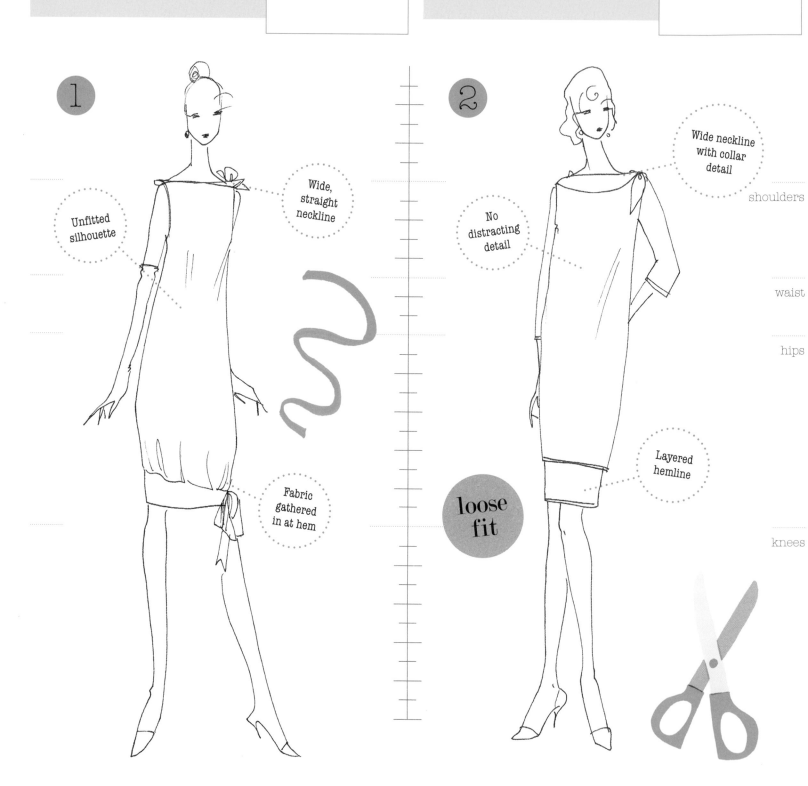

1

Unfitted silhouette

Wide, straight neckline

Fabric gathered in at hem

2

No distracting detail

Wide neckline with collar detail

shoulders

waist

hips

Layered hemline

loose fit

knees

Chemise dress

Draw each side of the collar so that it curves around the base of the neck. Join the collar at the front with a curved neckline. Add soft shoulders and sleeves.

Detail the armholes and continue the lines for the sides of the dress, tapering in towards the knees. Join up the narrow hem. Add the buttons.

CLOSE-UP

'Chemise' is another name for the sack dress. Many designers created variations of this shape in the 1950s and 1960s, including Yves Saint Laurent and Pierre Cardin.

Bazaar dress

Create the round neckline with tab and button details. Add shoulders, straight armholes and short sleeves.

Now draw the sides of the dress, joined by a straight hem below the knees. Add tab and button details to each side of the dress, just between the waist and hips of the croquis.

CLOSE-UP

In 1955, British designer Mary Quant opened the Bazaar fashion boutique in London. She sold dresses like this for younger women. Compare this shape with Quant's minis of the 1960s.

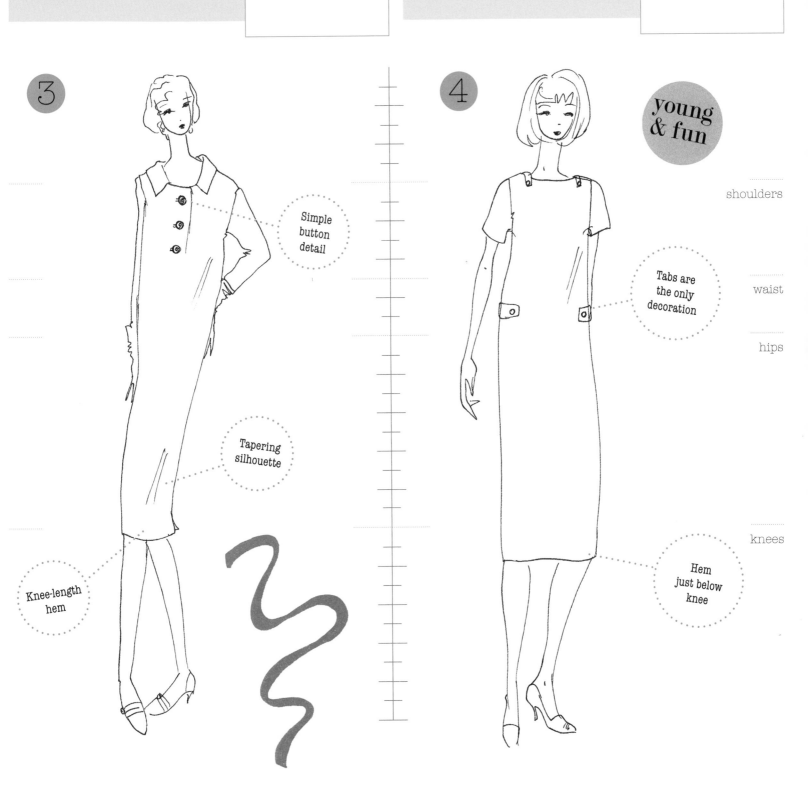

3

Simple button detail

Tapering silhouette

Knee-length hem

4

young & fun

shoulders

Tabs are the only decoration

waist

hips

knees

Hem just below knee

What's in the look?

Yellow and shocking pink towelling shift dress, 1967, designed by Foale and Tuffin
Photograph copyright Foale and Tuffin

In the 1960s, there was a growing number of teenagers with money to spend. A new generation of designers made bold, youthful and easy-to-wear clothes for them.

The 'mini-skirt' or 'mini-dress' was a key design. Typical features included an A-line shape, zip and pocket details, Pop Art graphics, Op Art black-and-white styling and creative use of new materials such as plastic, Perspex, paper and metal.

Minis and hot pants emphasise the legs and flatter a younger, boyish silhouette. To complement the look, French designer Pierre Cardin introduced thick, brightly coloured tights.

This towelling shift dress is by British designers Foale and Tuffin. Its simple shape and everyday fabric could not be more different from the formal, fitted tailoring of the 1950s (see pages 46–47).

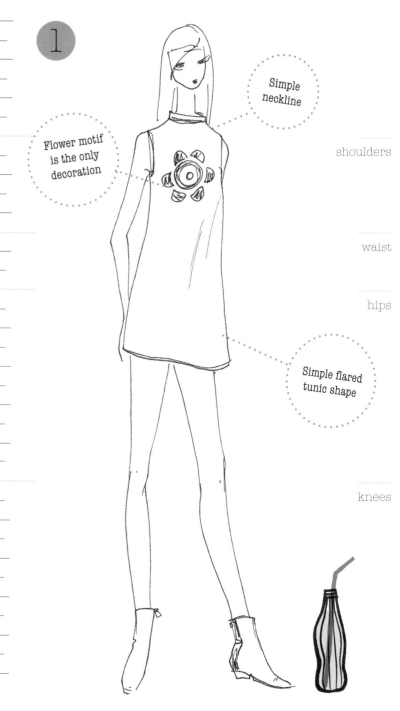

1

Flower motif is the only decoration

Simple neckline

shoulders

waist

hips

Simple flared tunic shape

knees

Sleeveless mini-dress

Create the high round neckline and the shoulders. Use similar detailing at the neck and armholes.

Let the silhouette of the dress fall in a flared shift shape, and add the hem.

Choose a motif to embellish the dress at the front.

CLOSE-UP

Many designers contributed to the invention of the mini-skirt. Try researching British designer Mary Quant, French designer André Courrèges and American designer Betsey Johnson, for example.

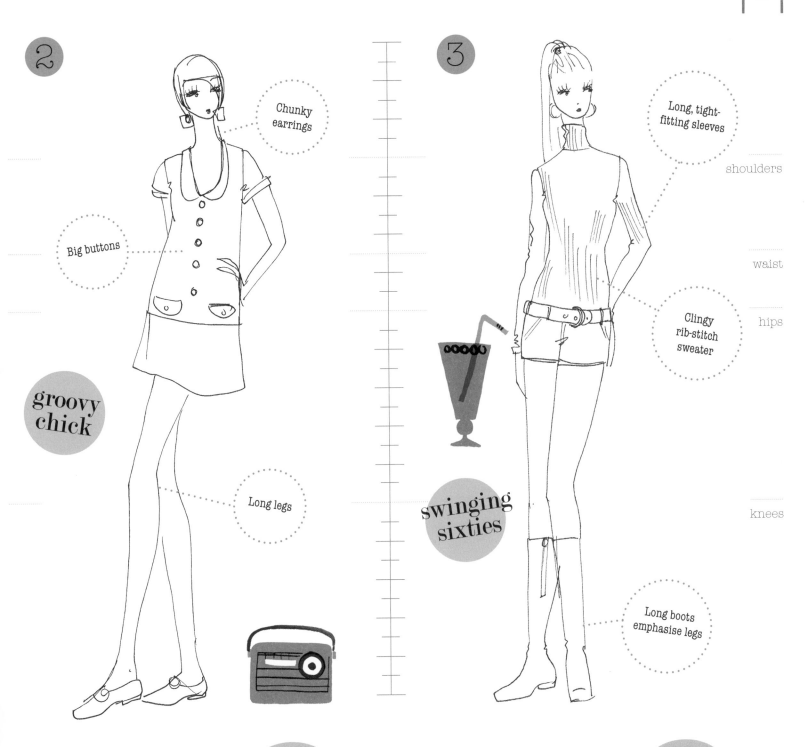

② groovy chick

Chunky earrings

Big buttons

Long legs

③ swinging sixties

Long, tight-fitting sleeves

shoulders

waist

hips

Clingy rib-stitch sweater

knees

Long boots emphasise legs

Babydoll dress

Start with the narrow scooped neck. Beneath this line draw both sides of the round collar.

Add shoulders, armholes and short, capped sleeves with a wide cuff.

Let the sides of the dress follow the line of the body, flaring towards the thighs. Join up the hem and add details such as the centre buttons, pockets and a line for the dropped waist.

CLOSE-UP

This style of dress was popular in the mid-1960s. It was suited to younger teenage girls who did not want to look like their mothers. The large collar, buttons and pockets created a very youthful image.

Hot pants and Poor Boy Sweater

Start with the Poor Boy Sweater. Draw the ribbed turtleneck. Add shoulders and armholes. Use a wiggly line to indicate where the tight sleeves have been pushed up the arm.

The belt sits low on the hips. Add the belt loops and draw the outline of the tight shorts. Detail the front opening and pockets.

To finish, add tight calf-high boots.

CLOSE-UP

Hot pants were an alternative to the mini-dress, and were often made in denim or suede. The Poor Boy Sweater was made popular in the 1960s by Parisian designer Sonia Rykiel. She is famous for her tight knitwear and boldly patterned fabrics.

Tunic dress

Start with the narrow opening of the keyhole neckline. Add the surrounding embroidered panel and shoulder lines.

Draw in the armholes and continue these lines to create the loose dress silhouette, flaring over the hips. Join up the hem to show movement. Add the sleeves, with embroidered details at the wide cuffs.

CLOSE-UP

This tunic takes inspiration from the kaftan – a traditional garment worn in Islamic cultures that became popular with hippies from the 1960s onwards. A kaftan would be full length.

Flower Power flares

Flared trousers, with low-slung hipster waistlines, became fashionable between the mid-1960s and 70s. Here, they are paired with a tight, cropped vest.

Start with the top, following the body closely. For the trousers, draw the wide waistband and belt and then closely follow the line of the legs, flaring the trousers out below the knee.

CLOSE-UP

The slogan 'Flower Power' refers to the flowers that hippies wore and handed out as an anti-war protest. Add flowers to this outfit – in the hair and as motifs on the garments.

1

Embroidered panels

Long beads

Fringed boots

2

Flower detail

Beaded fringing

feelin' groovy

Platform soles

shoulders

waist

hips

knees

Peasant dress

Draw the bodice, beginning with the round neck and teardrop opening. Add shoulders, deep armholes and a loose body gathered into a high, tight belt.

Create the long skirt with a frill at the hem. Add lines to suggest fullness. Now add fitted sleeves that open out at the elbow and gather in at the wrist. Use a scribbly line for the lace on the bodice and skirt.

CLOSE-UP

The term 'peasant' describes feminine dresses and blouses in cotton or fine fabrics, with simple, unstructured tailoring. Printed fabrics suggest other cultures.

Long waistcoat and hot pants

Start with the V neckline, narrow shoulders and inset armholes. Create the bodice with short sides and high waist, rising at the centre of the bust.

Drop two lines from the centre of the waist, widening out for the front opening. Add hot pants and legs, then complete the sides and hem of the coat.

CLOSE-UP

Typical hippy clothes have a hand-crafted feel. To create the hippy look, customise your designs with stitching, appliqué and decorative motifs.

3

Teardrop opening

Sleeves balloon out from the elbow

Full skirt with frill

4

far out!

Decorative stitching

Appliqué motifs

shoulders

waist

hips

knees

1

Ribbon sash

High ruffled bib

pretty pinny

2

Buttoned bodice

shoulders

waist

hips

Feminine flounces

knees

Buttoned boots

Pinafore day dress

Start with the high neckline and square bib shape of the pinafore. Imagine how this ties at the back. Add the high shoulder ruffles and frills at the seams of the bodice.

Draw the sleeves, widening towards the wrist and then gathering into an embellished cuff.

Create a full floor-length skirt. Add a curved hem with a frill. Remember the frill should stand away from the hem to make it look three-dimensional.

CLOSE-UP

This drawing is inspired by British designer Gina Fratini, who created romantic dresses worn by Princess Anne and Diana, Princess of Wales. Look at 1970s wedding dresses to further explore her influence.

Prairie dress

Start with the scooped neck, shoulders and armholes. Continue the line of the armhole to the waist, following the contours of the body tightly. Draw the arms with decorative frills at the wrist.

Add the waist. Hang the skirt's first ruffle from the waist. Add successive tiers of ruffles to just above the ankles.

Use accessories such as buttoned boots and a ribbon neck choker to add a historical flavour.

CLOSE-UP

The 'prairie' dress is named after the home-made skirts worn by women in the 19th-century American West. They were made of country-style fabrics such as denim or flowered calico. You could experiment with other fabrics in your designs.

③

High frilled collar

Long puffed sleeves

Long frilled and buttoned bib

sweet dreams

Edwardian-style tennis dress

Start with the high pleated neck. Add the shoulders and long oval bib, detailing the neat ruffle at the edge and a line of buttons at the placket.

Fill in the edges of the bodice and neat waist. Draw the puffed sleeves to stick out above the shoulder line and at the cuffs.

Hang the long skirt from the waist seam and flare gently below the knee. Use lines to show where the gathers and pleats of the fabric fall.

CLOSE-UP

This design is typical of Edwardian day dresses. Laura Ashley created a new version of this look that was very popular from the late 1960s onwards. How could you interpret this look for the 21st century?

What's in the look?

A model wears a white cotton frilly dress from Laura Ashley, 1974

From the 1950s to the 1970s, books, films and television series fuelled a yearning for a bygone era, and a romantic vision of Victorian and Edwardian fashions.

In the 1970s, many designers drew inspiration from the past and created their own interpretations of Victorian and Edwardian styles. These designers included Ossie Clark, Thea Porter, Giorgio de Sant' Angelo and Bill Gibb. Romantic bridalwear by Gina Fratini was especially popular. Hollywood star and style icon Elizabeth Taylor wore a Gina Fratini dress for her second marriage to Richard Burton. But it was perhaps British design firm Laura Ashley that identified themselves most strongly with 1970s nostalgia. Making it their trademark look, they went on to achieve international success.

Hallmarks of the style include floor-length dresses, pinafores, long skirts, feminine frills, high collars, fitted bodices, puffed sleeves, pleating, button fastenings and slightly transparent fabrics. The photograph above, used to advertise the Laura Ashley brand, captures this romantic, escapist look.

What's in the look?

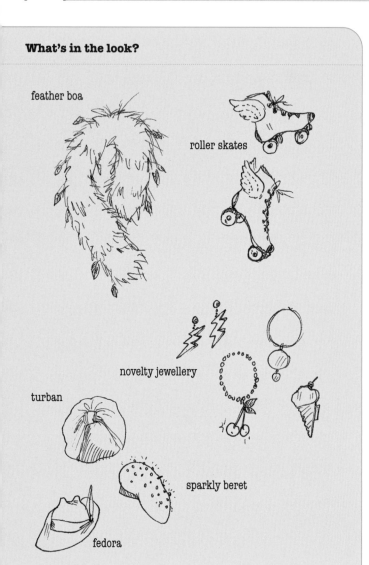

feather boa

roller skates

novelty jewellery

turban

sparkly beret

fedora

Disco music became popular in the 1970s. At first it was promoted in American nightclubs or discothèques, but by the late 1970s it had become the bestselling music genre in the world.

Disco dancing encouraged people to dress up and to show off their bodies in close-fitting clothes that could move with the music. From 1977, New York's most fashionable club was Studio 54. Dancers there typically wore flamboyant fabrics, including lurex, lamé, Lycra, silk, velvet and fur, plus feathers and sparkling sequins.

Hairstyles were also crucial to 1970s style – look at photos of the actresses and models Lauren Hutton, Farrah Fawcett, Jerry Hall, Janice Dickinson and Iman for ideas.

Silk jersey halter-neck dress

Use a typical 1970s croquis (see page 35). Draw a plunging neckline down from either side of the neck to below the bust. Draw the front panels over the bust. Imagine how these tie at the neck, exposing the shoulders.

Create the wide cummerbund belt. Add the bell-shaped skirt, ending it below the knee. Join up the hem, curving it in and out to show the fullness of fabric.

Use a typical 1970s croquis (see page 35).

CLOSE-UP

Halter-neck tops, which wrap around the neck to expose the upper back, became popular in the 1970s. Look up some designs by the fashion house Halston.

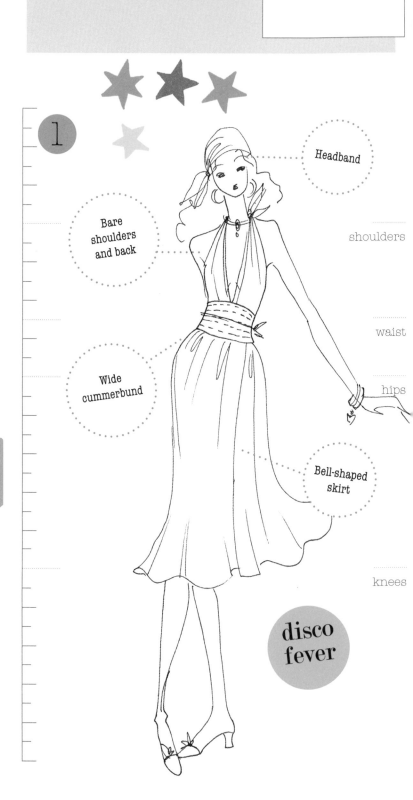

1

Headband

Bare shoulders and back

shoulders

Wide cummerbund

waist

hips

Bell-shaped skirt

knees

disco fever

Studio 54 playsuit

Start with the spaghetti straps, which join up above the bust and curve away under each arm.

Draw the loose bodice, which gathers in and pouches over the waistband. Use vertical squiggles to show how the fabric falls.

Add the knickerbocker trousers, with lines showing where the fabric gathers in a string tie at the knee.

CLOSE-UP

Spaghetti-strapped and tube tops were commonly seen in the 1970s. Look at dance clothing such as leotards and wrap skirts, which inspired the disco look.

Kensington dancing queen

Draw the cropped satin bustier with its sweetheart neckline, and add the flared shoulders.

Draw a narrow waistband and let the outline of the skirt follow the shape of the hips and legs until it flares slightly at the calf-length hem.

Add buttons and lines to the skirt and the top to show where the fabric pulls together.

CLOSE-UP

In the 1970s, boutiques such as Biba in London promoted young British fashion. This outfit is inspired by designs that Lee Bender sold in her Bus Stop boutique.

Big hair

Spaghetti straps

Loose fit for easy movement

Ankle-wrap shoes for dancing

Skimpy top

Bare midriff

move with the music

shoulders

waist

hips

knees

What's in the look?

Wedding dress by Zandra Rhodes, 1977

Punk style was connected with the punk rock music movement – and it aimed to shock. Punk fashion was first taken up by British teenagers in the 1970s. They customised everyday clothes, tearing them and decorating them with slogans.

Fashion designers responded to punk by featuring elements of the style in their collections. Vivienne Westwood sold ready-made punk-style garments in her London shop. In 1977, Zandra Rhodes created her 'Conceptual Chic' collection. It included many punk features, such as chains, slashed fabric and safety pins, but now the safety pins had jewels on them. This photograph by Clive Arrowsmith shows a wedding dress from that collection.

street fashion

Metal collar

shoulders

waist

hips

knees

Chunky boots

Mini-kilt and fishnet tights

Start with the slashed neckline of the sweater. Fill in the loose, lumpy outline of the top, adding fullness at the wrists to indicate oversized sleeves.

Draw the flap of the mini-kilt, adding pleats at the side. Add the industrial lace-up boots. Use crosshatching on the legs to illustrate the fishnet tights.

CLOSE-UP

This mixture of clothes has been sourced cheaply in keeping with the street-style origins of punk. What could you put together to create a punk outfit?

② Spikes and studs

③ Spiky hair

shoulders

waist

hips

Chains

Safety pins

girl with attitude

knees

Strappy, high-heeled boots

Bondage trousers

Start with the collar, drawing the lapels and front opening. Add the shoulders, armholes, edges and arms.

Draw the low-slung waistband and belt of the bondage trousers – so-called because of the straps that join the legs together.

CLOSE-UP

Customise your designs with punk motifs such as metal studs, chains and badges, or add slashes to the fabric for effect.

Punk chic

Start with the wide neckline, body and arms of the top. Draw small folds where the tight cloth gathers at the waist and elbow joints. Indicate a sheer fabric by outlining the camisole underneath.

Draw the studded belt curved around the hips, and the front flap of the skirt. Use small stress lines to indicate the tight leggings.

CLOSE-UP

Hair, jewellery and make-up all add to the punk look. Why not give your croquis spiked and coloured hair, for shock effect?

Rockabilly jeans

Look at the loose shape and the detailing of these oversized jeans. Details include the topstitching at the seams, the placket and the coin pocket, the wide turn-ups and the belt holding up the jeans.

Beatnik jeans

Start with the top: draw a wiggly neckline and add a frill below. Draw the curved waistband and trouser legs with plain turn-ups. Add detailing at pockets and a mark where the hidden placket ends.

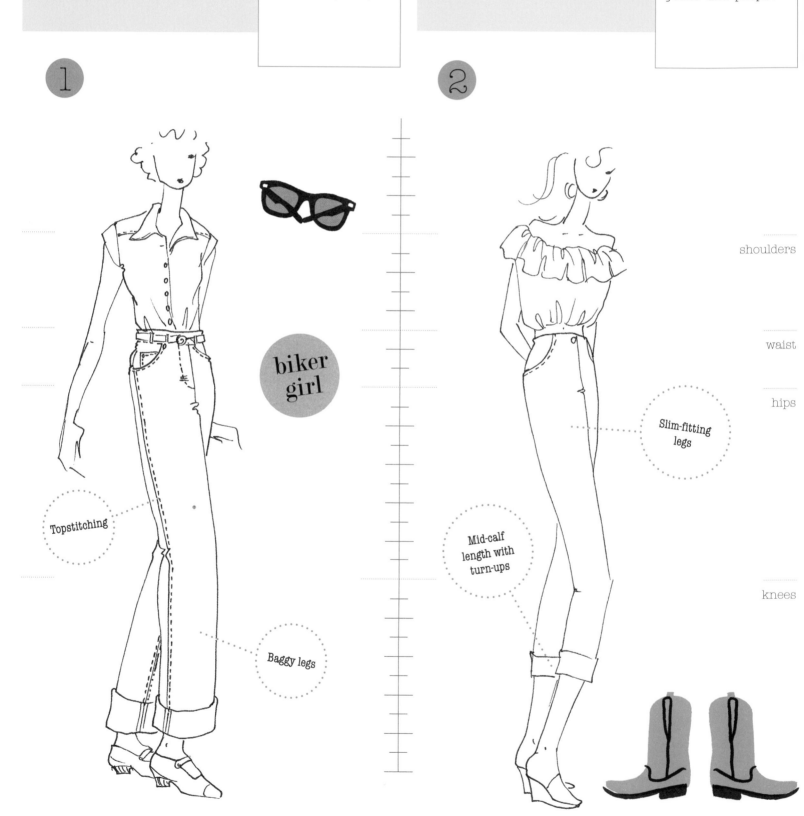

1

biker girl

Topstitching

Baggy legs

2

shoulders

waist

hips

Slim-fitting legs

Mid-calf length with turn-ups

knees

Designer flares

This silhouette, tight at the waist, hips and thighs then flaring below the knee, became popular in the 1970s. Note the sharp crease down each leg emphasising the lean silhouette.

CLOSE-UP

Traditional blue-jean labels include Levi's and Lee, but in the 1970s designer jeans arrived. Look at brands such as Gloria Vanderbilt.

Teen pop overalls

Start with the shoulder straps and front bib. Draw a line where the bib ends, and drop down straight lines for the wide trouser legs. Add buttons at the sides where the trousers open, and indicate the back of the overalls.

CLOSE-UP

Research images of some late 20th-century pop groups such as New Kids on the Block, B*Witched and S-Club 7. They all wore overalls.

3

4

1970s-style big hair

long & slinky

Dropped waist

Platform heels

shoulders

waist

hips

Loose, baggy fit

Wide legs

knees

①

Classic shoulder epaulettes

Double-breasted opening

screen goddess

②

Big sunglasses

Single-breasted opening

shoulders

waist

hips

Mini-length coat

knees

Knee-high boots

ooh la-la!

1940s 'swing' trenchcoat

Start with the collar and the wide notched lapels. Continue the left collar line across the body so that it becomes the coat opening.

Draw the square shoulders and the armholes. Gather the top of the coat into the belt, tied on the right with the buckle hanging down.

Add volume at the hips and hem to give the coat its 'swing'. Draw the arms and cuffs. Add details – deep pockets, topstitching on the collar and large buttons.

CLOSE-UP

The trench coat was created for men, but movie actresses helped to make it fashionable for women. This trenchcoat is based on one worn by Marlene Dietrich in the film *A Foreign Affair* (1948).

1960s New Wave

Start with the V-neckline. Add the collar with notched lapels and a striped top underneath. Draw the fitted shoulders and armholes.

Create the outline of the coat, tightly following the croquis to the thighs.

Add the curved hem, then the arms and the details of the coat. Detail the stitching on the upper bodice and pockets.

CLOSE-UP

In the 1960s, stars of French 'New Wave' cinema, such as Brigitte Bardot, Catherine Deneuve and Jean Seberg, wore short trenchcoats. The mini-length coat, sunglasses, summer top and boots were a bold combination at the time.

3

Storm flaps

Classic
trench coat
has 10 front
buttons

Contemporary trench coat

Draw the outer edge of the upturned collar first. Continue the inside collar line around the neck and down the front of the coat.

Add the shoulder straps and armholes, marking the edge of the front storm flaps. Draw the outline of the coat, following the croquis closely at the waist and hips.

Draw the belt and arms, and add the buttons and topstitching hem details.

CLOSE-UP

This 'vintage' look dates from the 1990s. During this decade Burberry promoted its heritage brand by placing famous models in classic trench coats in a high-profile advertising campaign.

What's in the look?

Contemporary trench coat styled and worn by model Bruna Tenório. Paris Fashion Week, March 2011. Photograph by Kirstin Sinclair

The trench coat is considered a design classic: a functional overcoat that is usually double-breasted, belted, buttoned and made from weatherproof fabric.

Today the trench coat features in many fashion collections but it began as a military garment. The trenchcoat was made from gabardine – a closely woven cloth patented in 1883 – and provided a lighter alternative to the traditional army greatcoat. After World War I ended, the trenchcoat became popular with civilians.

British companies, including Aquascutum and Burberry, claim that they invented this classic coat. The style is also associated with the Scottish Mackintosh, or raincoat, which is made from rubberised fabric.

During the 20th century, the trench coat was adapted by high-profile designers, notably Yves Saint Laurent in 1962 and Halston in 1972. Today it features in many designer and high-street collections, in lots of varieties.

What's in the look?

Cocktail dress in black cloqué, designed by David Sassoon and worn by model Avril Humphries, 1957

The Little Black Dress – also known as the LBD – is an essential fashion item. It can be worn in the day or dressed up with accessories for the evening.

The idea for the LBD dates from 1926, when French fashion designer Coco Chanel first showcased a simple black jersey dress in American *Vogue*. The magazine predicted that it would be as popular as Henry Ford's Model T Car and nicknamed it the 'Chanel Ford'. They were right – the LBD has remained a favourite ever since.

After World War II, cocktail parties grew in popularity and the LBD was seen as the perfect 'cocktail dress'. When actress Audrey Hepburn wore it, with pearls and sunglasses, in the 1961 film *Breakfast at Tiffany's*, the garment became a style icon. The challenge for contemporary designers is how to update this classic.

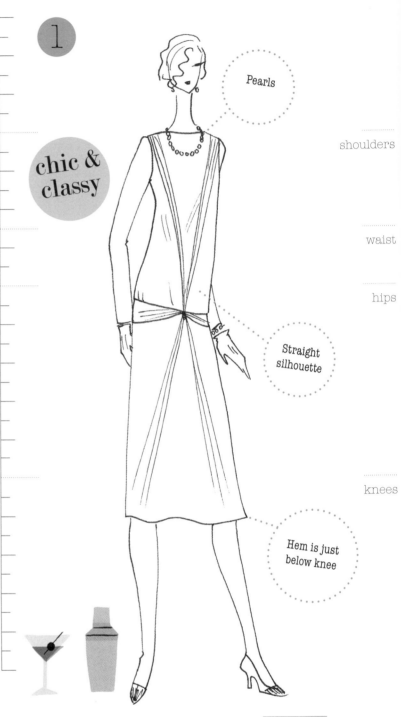

1

chic & classy

Pearls

shoulders

waist

hips

Straight silhouette

knees

Hem is just below knee

1920s 'Chanel Ford' dress

Draw the straight neckline across and out to each shoulder. Add gently curved armholes. Draw the sides of the dress down to the hips, and add a line from one hip to the other for the sash.

Detail pintucks in a V-shape from each shoulder into the middle of the sash. Curve the base of the sash upwards into the same point. Create the slim A-line skirt with pleats flaring out from the centre to mirror those in the top. Add simple sleeves.

CLOSE-UP

This is a typical 1920s day dress in the style of the French fashion designer Coco Chanel. For authentic Chanel style, you could also add gloves and a little hat (see pages 50–51).

2

Dropped, gathered waistline

sixties chic

Band of feathers near hem

Hem falls just on knee

3

Fitted waistline with darts

shoulders

waist

hips

Mini-length skirt

knees

1961 Holly Golightly dress

For the neckline, draw a line across from one shoulder to the other. Add bow details at the shoulder and drop two lines for the armholes.

Draw the sides of the dress gathering into a dropped waist. Use lines to show where the fabric gathers.

Hang the skirt from the dropped waistline. Draw the feathered frill above the knee, and add the soft waves of the hemline.

CLOSE-UP

This sketch is inspired by a dress worn by Audrey Hepburn when she played Holly Golightly in the 1961 film *Breakfast at Tiffany's*. The dress was designed by Hubert de Givenchy.

1970s jersey tea dress

Create a deep V neckline and add the shoulders. Draw short sleeves that rise out of the armholes with tight pleats, before narrowing and then flaring above the elbows.

Draw the tight, high waist, then give the bodice loose sides, gathering these into the waist. Let the outline of the skirt follow the shape of the hips before flaring out at the thighs.

Draw the hem with a number of curves to show the fullness of fabric.

CLOSE-UP

The heyday of the LBD was the 1950s and 1960s - but vintage styles are constantly being reinvented. Look at 1930s dresses and you will see how they have influenced this drawing, which is based on the 1970s dresses designed by Lee Bender.

1900s tunic dress

Start with the high collar and shoulderline. Add frills at the armholes. Draw the blouse bodice, keeping this full at the bustline and ribs and then gathering it into the tight waist.

Complete the full puffed sleeves and buttoned cuffs. Draw the yoke of the skirt, with its point marking a central pleat. Add the A-line skirt sides and curve the hem into the main pleat.

CLOSE-UP

Look at Charles Dana Gibson's drawings of his 'Gibson Girl'. She was seen as one of the 'New Women' – modern, sporty and fashionable.

1940s McCardell shirtwaister

Draw the V-shaped neckline and the soft shirt lapels around it. Continue the inside line of the left lapel down the front of the dress.

Add the loose shoulders and sleeves and create the wide cloth cummerbund. Gather the bodice and add the full skirt with pleats above and below the waist. Create a loose wavy hem and add buttons down the centre opening.

CLOSE-UP

Adapt your design depending on whether it is for daywear or a party. Common fabrics include cotton, linen, gingham and denim. What effect might silk, or a stiffer fabric, have on your design?

Swept-up hair reveals neckline

Tiny waist

Buttoned boots

Wide cummerbund at waist

Shirt-style button-through opening

shoulders

waist

hips

knees

cool classic

1970s Halston shirt dress

Draw the outside edge of the collar on the left. Continue the inside edge down the centre of the bodice to the waistline. Draw the other side of the collar to create a narrow V-shaped neckline.

Add the shoulders and continue the armholes down to create the bodice. Add a fabric belt and gentle A-line skirt. Finish with patch pockets, turned-up sleeves and buttons.

CLOSE-UP

Vary this classic style with details such as pockets. Adjust the length of the skirt for different periods: 1940s (below the knee), 1950s (calf-length), 1960s (thigh-length) or 1970s (above the knee).

3

easy dressing

Casual tied cloth belt

Patch-pocket detail

Turned-up cuffs

What's in the look?

'Horrockses Fashion in Fine Cotton', advertisement, *Vogue*, June 1960

The shirtwaister, or shirtwaist dress, began in the late 19th century as a blouse with a high collar secured with buttons or a bow. The blouse was worn tucked into a long, high-waisted skirt, to emphasise a curvy silhouette. It was commonly worn by middle-class, working women from the 1880s to 1910s.

The shirtwaist silhouette did not suit the longer, lean lines of the 1920s but was adapted as a dress by American designers from the 1930s onwards. Claire McCardell, in particular, became known for her versatile button-through, knee-length shirtwaister dresses.

During the 1940s and 1950s, the shirtwaister was adjusted to feature longer, fuller skirts for party wear. It was reinvented in the 1970s. Roy Halston Howick made chic button-though day dresses, typically in khaki, and Diane von Furstenberg developed her signature wrap dress based on earlier shirtwaister styles. The dresses above show another adaptation of the shirtwaister shape.

1 express yourself!

Crosshatching shows string texture

Bangles and jewellery

Ra-ra skirt ruffles

Layered legwear

2 Camisole worn as outerwear

Thrift-store jewellery

Fingerless gloves

Lacy socks

shoulders

waist

hips

knees

Inside-outside

CLOSE-UP

Draw the straps, heart-shaped neckline and tight bodice of the bustier. Add the wide neck, shoulders and square shape of the string vest.

Draw the low, narrow waistband of the mini-skirt, followed by lots of frills. Follow the body croquis for the leggings, suggesting a tight fold of fabric at the knee.

Complete the look with crucifix jewellery, rubber bracelets, fishnet tights, leg warmers and spiky boots.

Music videos from the 1980s had a huge influence on how people dressed. This look is based on pop star Madonna's image in 1983. Her style at this time featured lacy leggings, mini-skirts, off-the-shoulder tops and bangles.

Fun girl

CLOSE-UP

Begin with the bodice, adding multiple bra and camisole straps. Decorate the neckline with a frill.

A long belt wraps around the waist and hips. Draw the left side of the skirt curving around the hip and flaring out above the knee in a frill.

Create the ruffled hem, starting at the right hip. Use a wavy line to show how the top layer cascades across the body to meet the hem at the other side. Add another layer beneath this.

Lingerie worn as outerwear was a big 1980s trend. This outfit is inspired by singer Cyndi Lauper, who had a hit with the song 'Girls Just Want to Have Fun'. Also, look at the character played by Molly Ringwald in the movie *Pretty in Pink* (1986).

3

Suspenders (one worn inside sweater)

Baggy trousers

Lace-up loafers

4

Big hoop earrings

Brooches

cool California

shoulders

waist

hips

knees

Art school apparel

Starting on the left side, draw the edge of the collar that is peeking over the sweater.

Add the sweater's wide V-neck and sleeves. Finish each sleeve with a turned-up cuff. Draw the waistband and wide trouser legs with cuffs.

Finish off with a hat, shoes and suspenders, with one strap inside the sweater and another outside it.

CLOSE-UP

```
In the 1980s
British female pop
trio Bananarama
made this tomboy
style popular.
They combined
denim and workwear,
such as baggy
jeans and
lace-up boots,
with spiky
haircuts and
bold make-up.
```

Dressy denim jacket

Use a nice sharp line for the collar, shoulders and armholes of the short jacket. Draw the front opening of the jacket and the angled pockets, then complete the sleeves. Use dotted lines for the topstitching.

Using squiggles, suggest the texture of the dress beneath, concentrating on the silhouette and hem.

Complete the look with lace-edged leggings and spiky stiletto boots.

CLOSE-UP

```
This outfit is
styled to reflect
the look of the
all-female guitar
group The Bangles.
The band often
dressed in black
but pink, yellow,
turquoise and lime
green were also
popular during
the decade. Think
about colour in
your own design.
```

What's in the look?

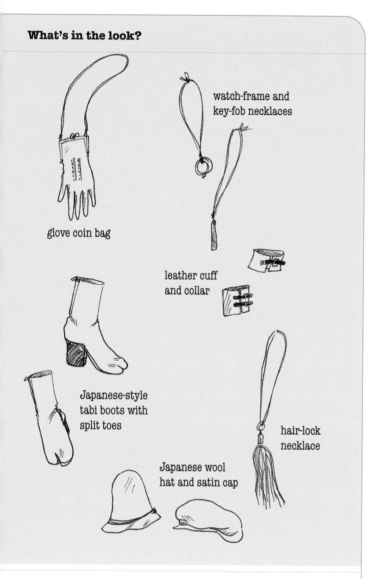

glove coin bag

watch-frame and key-fob necklaces

leather cuff and collar

Japanese-style tabi boots with split toes

hair-lock necklace

Japanese wool hat and satin cap

'Intellectual chic', 'post-nuclear fashion', 'Modernist' and 'wearable art' are all terms that describe the work of Japanese designers Rei Kawakubo, Yohji Yamamoto and Issey Miyake. All of them began to show their collections in Europe in the early 1980s.

Their designs emphasise the silhouette and play with oversized proportions and unconventional finishes such as distressed fabrics and unfinished seams. Accessories often show their Japanese origin.

Black is a favourite colour. The designers' skilled construction techniques almost make it look as if a garment has literally been taken apart – or 'deconstructed'. Their approach created a wholly new 'look' for fashion in the 1980s.

In Belgium at the same time, another group of designers had a similar approach. Martin Margiela, and the group of his contemporaries known as the 'Antwerp Six', explored ideas such as deconstruction, recycling existing garments and materials and including deliberate imperfections.

Hiroshima bag lady

Draw the rough curved neckline of the sweater and baggy sleeves. Add wide turn-up cuffs and a rough hem.

Continue the skirt down the body, adding gathers and pleats. Create the skirt's uneven hemline.

Use sketchy marks to loosely describe the separate elements on the sweater, with ribbing at the neck, hem and cuffs.

CLOSE-UP

Look at the designs that Rei Kawakubo showed in Paris in 1981, under her Comme des Garçons label. Her monochrome colours, unpicked threads and unfinished seams introduced a whole new look.

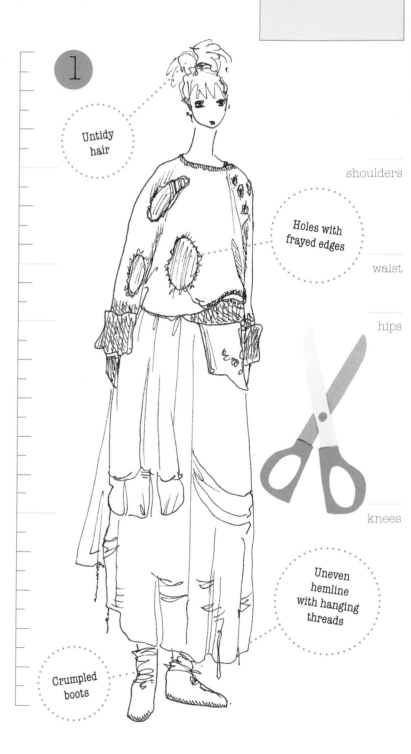

1

Untidy hair

shoulders

Holes with frayed edges

waist

hips

knees

Uneven hemline with hanging threads

Crumpled boots

Tokyo modern

Start with the neat high collar and shirt placket followed by the soft shoulders and upper arms of the jacket. Drop down two lines for the jacket opening, and shape the jacket around the body.

Detail the cut, pleats and ruched material of the shirt, then join up the curved hem.

Follow the outline of the legs for the skirt. Join up the hem at a gentle angle.

CLOSE-UP

Explore the designs of Yohji Yamamoto. His clever draping, layering, pleating, cutting, patches of colour and asymmetrical silhouettes are now admired worldwide.

Tied top and maxi-skirt

Start with the tight neckline, shoulders and capped sleeve details.

Draw the oversized armlets and frayed sleeves. Add the sides and cropped seam of the top tunic.

Continue the sides of the tunic to the hips, pulling it in at the waist with linen laces. Draw the hem across the body. Continue the skirt to the feet, with a centre seam and slit.

CLOSE-UP

This outfit is inspired by the work of Martin Margiela. He created a design with exaggerated proportions and visible construction details, such as seams on the outside.

2

Loose, floppy beret

Long, loose layers

Elongated silhouette

Boots left unlaced

3

String necklace

Waist pulled in with laces

Tie-on sleeves

Inside-out darts

shoulders

waist

hips

long & lean

knees

Japanese-style tabi boots

1

Bias cut clings to the body

2

Strapless top

Long gloves

Wide sash emphasises hourglass figure

shoulders

waist

hips

knees

screen goddess

Slinky siren

Draw two straps from the inside of each shoulder to just above the bust.

Draw a curved line between the straps for the neckline, with a lace detail. Continue the outer edge of each strap under the arms.

Draw in the silhouette of the dress to follow the shape of the body, flaring out at the hem with a train on one side. Use diagonal seams to show the bias-cut and construction.

CLOSE-UP

This style of dress was popular in the 1930s. 'Bias cut' means that the fabric is cut across the grain at a diagonal to give it stretch and movement. This technique shows off the figure.

Gilda's gown

Use a 1940s or 1950s croquis (see page 33 or 34). The pose, with weight on the rear leg and hands on hips, emphasises the curves of the dress.

Draw the sweetheart neckline and the sides of the strapless bodice, tightening in towards the waist. Add a wide sash across the body, with a large bow to one side.

Complete the fitted skirt to emphasise the front leg. Use bust darts and lines to highlight the direction of the fabric.

CLOSE-UP

Explore the work of Hollywood costume designers. Jean Louis designed a dress like this one for Rita Hayworth in the film Gilda (1946). William Travilla created Marilyn Monroe's famous hot-pink gown in Gentleman Prefer Blondes (1953).

3

film-star style

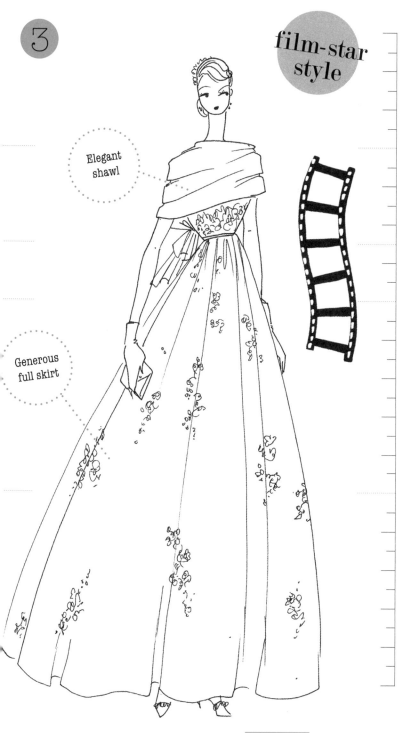

Elegant shawl

Generous full skirt

Glamorous Grace

Start with the shawl, beginning with a straight line that runs from right to left and curves around the left side of the croquis.

Draw in the lower part of the bodice with a tight waistline. Hang the full long skirt from this line, with wide folds of fabric.

Add details such as embroidery and wrist-length gloves.

CLOSE-UP

This elegant and glamorous look is inspired by the actress Grace Kelly, who starred in Hollywood films in the 1950s. Research the work of Edith Head, who dressed Grace Kelly both on- and off-screen.

What's in the look?

Hand-embroidered, gold bead couture dress made for Madonna, 1999, by Bellville Sassoon Lorcan Mullany

The heyday of the classic Hollywood stars lasted from the 1930s to the 1950s. Hollywood glamour is usually associated with actresses such as Jean Harlow, Rita Hayworth and Marilyn Monroe. These women are sometimes called 'screen sirens' because of their glamour and allure. Costume designers helped to create a distinct look for each star.

Sometimes fashion designers work on films or make clothes for individual actresses. Coco Chanel went to Hollywood in the 1930s. Jean Paul Gaultier has worked with film directors Peter Greenaway, Luc Besson and Pedro Almodóvar.

The idea of Hollywood glamour has been revived in recent years for red-carpet events, such as film premieres, award ceremonies and exhibition openings. These occasions give designers a chance to showcase their work and to associate themselves with high-profile actresses, models and musicians. The dress above was designed for Madonna to wear to an event in 1999.

What's in the look?

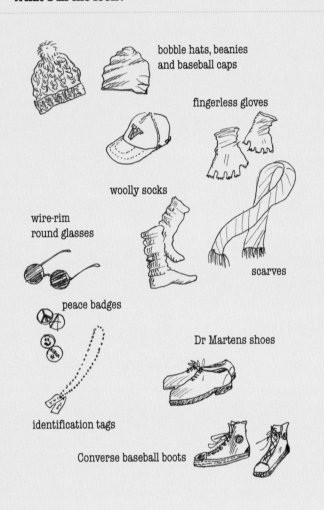

bobble hats, beanies and baseball caps

fingerless gloves

woolly socks

wire-rim round glasses

scarves

peace badges

Dr Martens shoes

identification tags

Converse baseball boots

'Grunge' is the name of the alternative rock music that emerged in the Seattle area of North America in the late 1980s. It is most closely linked with the big, gritty guitar sound of bands such as Nirvana and Pearl Jam.

Grunge is one of the most important style ideas of the 1990s and continues to influence designers today. Yet the grunge look is essentially 'anti-fashion' – the very opposite of haute couture. In unexpected combinations, scruffy workwear is worn with softer, more feminine pieces. So rough-and-tough jeans, boots, T-shirts, oversized sweaters and lumberjack shirts may be paired with long, floaty skirts or pretty babydoll dresses. Dishevelled hair and make-up are also part of the look.

Seattle slip dress

Start with the collar and open front of the lumberjack shirt. Add shoulders, frayed armholes and sides.

Draw the V-shaped, buttoned neckline of the dress. Continue the outline of the dress where the sides of the shirt end. Join up the hem above the ankles.

Add work boots and sketch some of the floral pattern on the dress.

Lumberjack shirt

Frayed, cut-off sleeves

shoulders

waist

hips

Floaty floral dress

knee

Heavy work boots

1

Babydoll dress

Denim jackets need lots of detailing to emphasise the raised seams and stitching. Draw the outline first, then the yoke, pockets and seams.

Add the neck and empire line of the babydoll dress, with a centre frill. Draw the dress outline and join up the hem. Follow the croquis closely for the cycling shorts.

CLOSE-UP

For more inspiration, research images of models Stella Tennant, Kristen McMenamy and Kate Moss. Their waif-like look was linked to the grunge style.

Lacy ruffled dress

Use a tight wavy line for the scooped neckline and straps of the bodice. Add the sides, with a vertical row of buttons and some lacy embellishment. Draw the fringed silk belt with a droopy bow at its centre.

Complete the skirt, drawing it down to mid-thigh. Add a tight wavy hem and vertical pleats to suggest a light chiffon fabric.

CLOSE-UP

This look has pretty, almost princess-like elements, but with a harder edge. Which details create the tougher side of grunge style?

Sound City

2

Frilly edges

Rolled-down stockings and high-top sneakers

Princess-style tiara

3

Fingerless gloves

come as you are

shoulders

waist

hips

knees

Ankle socks

Feminine scooped neckline

Beautifully cut jacket

Simple trousers

less is more

shoulders

waist

hips

knees

Simple silhouette and clean lines

Slip-on sandals

Urban slouchy suit

Draw the slim lapels, accentuated shoulders and fitted sleeves of the jacket. Continue the lapel lines for the jacket opening. Use diagonal lines on either side for the cropped hem.

Add the scooped, draped neckline of the top. Draw in the shirt opening and small buttons.

Imagine the trousers hanging from the waistband beneath the shirt. Draw a line for the placket opening. Fill in the silhouette loosely around the hips, and straight down the outline of each leg.

CLOSE-UP

This drawing is inspired by the designs of Helmut Lang, who combines sharp tailoring with high-tech fabrics. His original ideas are sometimes compared to those of the Japanese designers on pages 76-77.

Fluid sweater and skirt

Use a gentle curve for the neckline of the sweater. Add the shoulders and armholes. Continue the line of each armhole down to the hips, following the outline of the bust.

Add long sleeves and suggest folds of fabric around the waist.

Drop two lines down from the hem of the sweater for the straight skirt. Add stress lines on one side of your croquis where the leg joins the hip.

CLOSE-UP

Look at pictures of German designer Jil Sander's work in the 1980s and 1990s. Consider the different silhouettes she creates. Note how using a single colour emphasises the shape and silhouette of an outfit.

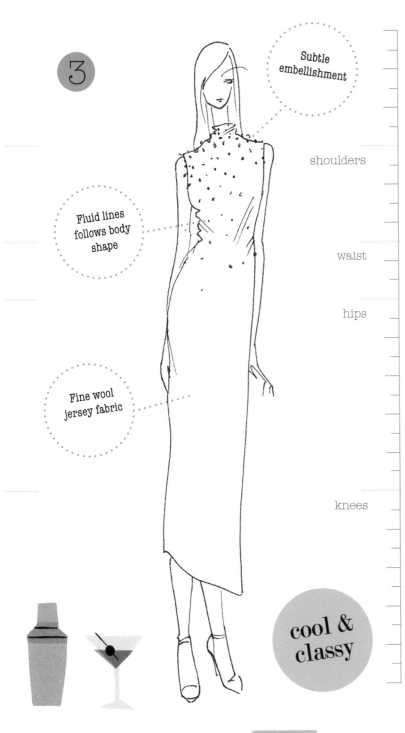

3

Subtle
embellishment

shoulders

Fluid lines
follows body
shape

waist

hips

Fine wool
jersey fabric

knees

cool &
classy

Black shift dress

Draw the high turtleneck and soft
shoulderline to just inside the
shoulders.

Continue the armholes straight down
and gather the sides around the
contours of the bust. Use a wavy line at
the sides of the ribcage and stress lines
to show where the fabric gathers and is
drawn tight across the body.

Continue the sides of the dress, curving
smoothly around the hips and dropping
straight down to the calves. Join up the
sides with an asymmetric hem.

CLOSE-UP

This fine wool
jersey dress is in
the classic style
of Calvin Klein.
In the 1990s,
Klein opted for a
limited palette
of colours in a
range of natural
fabrics. How might
this design look
in a material
such as silk or
leather?

What's in the look?

Calvin Klein womenswear 2010, New York, February 2010
Photograph by Kirstin Sinclair

The understated 'Minimalist Modernist' look is in
stark contrast to the flashy style of other 1990s
designers such as Gianni Versace, Jean Paul Gaultier
and Christian Lacroix. In fashion, minimalism
means clean lines, exquisite cut, neutral colours,
luxury fabric and restrained proportions. Garments
are pared back to focus on essentials. Buttons are
hidden, decoration is removed, and the construction
of the garment is made as invisible as possible.

These characteristics became popular in fashion
in the late 1980s and early 1990s. They are
especially associated with the work of Calvin Klein,
Helmut Lang and Jil Sander. By taking urban trends
such as layering, combined with skilled cutting and
expensive materials, these designers created a look
that was simple, elegant and futuristic at the same
time. Their work is also known as 'utilitarian'.

Minimalism was not restricted to fashion. Look
at the work of architects John Pawson and Claudio
Silvestrin, early issues of the magazine *Wallpaper*
(launched in 1996), and the 1997 science-fiction
film *Gattaca*.

Out and about

Fashion constantly reinvents the past.
Designers often look at historical dress
and period style for inspiration.
But how do they research their ideas?
Here are places where you might
discover your own source material.

 ①

 ②

③

MUSEUMS

Collections within museums
• Museums and galleries with
  dress collections allow you to
  see vintage garments in detail.

Major collections
• Museums with major collections
  of international significance
  include **The Costume Institute**
  at the Metropolitan Museum
  of Art in New York – with over
  35,000 items – and the **Victoria
  & Albert Museum** in London.

Local history museums
• Your local history museum
  may also have a collection or
  archive to visit. Do some **initial
  research** in books and online
  to find out about it. If garments
  are not on display, they may be
  on loan to another venue or in
  storage. You may need to book
  an appointment with a **curator**
  to see items in the archive.

AROUND THE WORLD

Specialist museums
There are many museums around
the world that are dedicated solely
to fashion. You may be able to visit
them if you are travelling or on
vacation there. Here are some to
start with:
• Cristóbal Balenciaga Museoa,
  Getaria, Spain
• Fashion Institute of Technology,
  New York
• Fashion and Textile Museum,
  London
• Fashion Museum, Bath, England
• FIDM (Fashion Institute of
  Design and Merchandising)
  Museum & Galleries,
  Los Angeles
• The Kyoto Costume Institute,
  Japan
• ModeMuseum (MoMu), Antwerp,
  Belgium
• ModeMuseum, Hasselt, Belgium
• Musée Galliera, Paris
• Museo de la Moda, Santiago,
  Chile
• Musée de la Mode et du Textile
  at the Louvre, Paris
• Musée des Arts Decoratifs et de
  la Mode, Marseilles, France
• New Zealand Fashion Museum
  www.nzfashionmuseum.org.nz
  has no permanent location but
  organises exhibitions in venues
  around the country

EXHIBITIONS

What's on show?
• With interest in fashion growing,
  more museums and galleries
  are keen to create relevant
  exhibitions and **displays**. Find
  out what is happening near you
  that might prove inspiring.

Individual designers
Exhibitions are a good way to
explore **different vintage periods**
and to study **specific designers'
work**, such as the following:
• The **Alexander McQueen**
  Savage Beauty exhibition at the
  Metropolitan Museum in 2011 –
  staged just after the designer's
  death – had over 650,000
  visitors and was one of its most
  popular shows ever.
• The **Vivienne Westwood**
  exhibition, organised by the
  Victoria and Albert Museum
  in 2004, has since travelled
  to 10 international venues.

④

ON STAGE

Theatre, ballet and opera
- Going to a play, ballet or opera can inspire ideas for **vintage looks**. If a production has a **period setting**, this will have been carefully researched and crafted by a team of people, including the costume designer.
- Study the **detail** of the costumes, and watch to see **how the clothes move** when worn.

Period style
- Go to see performances **set in the period** in which you are interested.
- If you cannot go to a live performance, you can still check out the costumes designed for it. If you are researching **1950s style**, for example, find images of the Broadway musical *Coco* (1969), in which Katharine Hepburn starred as the designer Chanel. The costumes were created by Cecil Beaton, the photographer and Oscar-winning designer.

⑤

SHOPS AND SALES

Vintage shops
- These shops offer a fantastic opportunity to learn about the history of fashion. They allow you to see close-up **how clothes were made** and to **try them on**.
- Be careful to distinguish what is **truly 'vintage'** from **second-hand** and **retro** clothing. It is possible to find lots of bad examples of old clothing as well as reproductions of older styles.

Street markets
- Wherever you go in the world, you can find examples of clothing from the past on sale. In some cities there are **specialist street markets** as well as **vintage retailers**.
- If you are interested in buying **vintage couture**, look for labels to distinguish proper couture from designer ready-to-wear. You can always ask the seller about the origins of a garment.

Auction houses
These are another useful place to study **clothes, accessories** and **jewellery** at close hand. Items are usually on display before each major sale so that people can see and handle them.

At home

Studying an actual historical garment is the most direct kind of research. But it is possible to find inspiration close at hand, too – descriptions of clothes in books and images of how they were worn, for example. Here are some ways you can research ideas at home.

BOOKS

Fashion and photography books

• These can provide new insights into the **history of design** as well as how clothes were worn.
• Study the **pictures** of the clothes you like in detail. Look at the poses of the models, as well as their accessories, to learn how you might capture the style.

Clothes in literature

• **Classic novels** may include inspiring descriptions of their characters' clothes.
• The **memoirs** and **biographies** of designers also provide fresh ways of thinking about their work.

Classic fashion books

Some of these classics may be available only in second-hand stores, but others have been reprinted for the 21st century.
• *The Glass of Fashion* by Cecil Beaton (1954)
• *The Little Dictionary of Fashion: A Guide to Dress Sense for Every Woman* by Christian Dior (1954)
• *What Shall I Wear? The What, Where, When and How Much of Fashion* by Claire McCardell (1956)
• *Mrs 'Arris Goes to Paris* by Paul Gallico (1958)
• *How to Dress for Success* by Edith Head (1967)

MAGAZINES

Which decade?

Some of today's most famous titles were founded over 100 years ago. Their pages chart the different moods, styles and designers of each decade. Magazine advertisements give you a good feeling for the **style of the times**. Find out which publications were most popular during the period you are interested in.
• Full runs of magazines are usually only available in **libraries**, but look out for individual copies in **second-hand bookshops**, too.

Influential magazines

Here are some you could explore:
• *Vogue* was founded in the USA in 1892 and now has over 20 editions worldwide. It has been called the world's most influential fashion magazine.
• *Harper's Bazaar* was first published in the USA in the 19th century. It was particularly influential in the 1940s and 1950s.
• *Elle* was founded in 1945 in France, and then launched in the USA and UK in the 1980s.
• *Womenswear Daily*, the American retail style bible, became popular in the 1960s.
• *Nova* was launched in the UK in 1965, and had a creative and experimental approach.

TELEVISION

Period drama

• The costumes and characters in period dramas can provide useful information and inspiration for your designs.

History and news

• Seek out history programmes where you can see **historical footage** and **still photographs** of particular periods.
• **News footage** was generally black and white until the 1970s, so you may need to refer to magazines to see the colour of certain garments.

Checking for accuracy

• Be careful about the types of programme you use for your research. Remember that television costume from any period is always an **interpretation** of how clothes might have looked. Even though the designs are usually carefully researched, they may be **influenced by modern taste**.
• Compare **newsreels** with a **modern drama set in the past** to see how the costume designers have interpreted the clothes for a 21st-century production.

④

⑤

ON THE WEB

Online sources
• The internet is an incredible resource not only for images of vintage garments, but also for advice on where to see them, read about them and even buy them.
• Online sources that are unique to the internet include **video sites** where you can see **historical newsreel footage**, museum and university **archives**, and **blogs** by fashion experts and designers.

Social media
• You may also use social media to **pose questions** about vintage items that you are unable to find answers to elsewhere.

Widen your search
• Features in digital magazines, mentions on social media and online photo essays may spark your interest, but note that information online is rarely comprehensive. You may need to scroll through **different search engines** and visit many **different sites** to get a fuller sense of any particular period.

FILMS

At the movies
• Watching films – whether in the cinema or at home – is a great, enjoyable way to research vintage looks. Old films show how particular clothes and accessories were styled and worn in certain periods.

Choose your period
Whatever the year, you will be able to find a film and character whose clothes reflect what was popular at the time.
• For **Edwardian costume**, for example, you could watch the movie musicals *Gigi* (1958) and *My Fair Lady* (1963). The costumes were created by Cecil Beaton.
• Compare costumes in **remakes** of the same film. For example, in 1940 Katharine Hepburn played the part of Tracy Samantha Lord, a wealthy socialite, in *The Philadelphia Story*. In 1956, Grace Kelly played the same part in a remake of the film, this time called *High Society*. Their dress styles reflect the different looks of the two periods.

Sketchbooks and moodboards

Think about how to record and save your vintage fashion ideas, images and information. You may want to revisit ideas in the future. How will you organise your research – by designer, date or type of garment?

Use your sketchbook to record vintage clothing that interests you. Sketching an outfit on a dress stand can help you to better understand its shape, proportions and construction details.

- Great ideas are often developed through **observational drawing**. Connections between the **work of one designer and another** might be revealed. As you work, other ideas can spring to mind.

- As you sketch, try to isolate **particular details** that you can refer back to when making a later design drawing or a finished illustration. These sketches are essential **reference tools** if you are working in museums or archives where photography is forbidden.

- Your sketchbook is your **private space**. Put whatever you like in it. It doesn't matter if you later think it is good or bad – the important thing is to understand **why you find it interesting**. By recording it, you will be able to remember your initial connection and use this feeling later.

- Express your ideas in **different ways**. You can collage illustrations and photographs, stick in newspaper articles, or write facts, notes and names to refer back to.

- There are many **shapes and sizes** of sketchbook. Experiment and find one that you are happy to carry with you at all times, and a format that you feel comfortable working with in most places. Your sketchbook might be small or large, portrait, landscape or square in shape, perfect-bound or spiral-bound, with sheets of cartridge or rice paper.

- Try to use your sketchbook **every day**.

This designer uses his sketchbook to record his ideas

You may choose a ring-bound, portrait-shaped sketchbook like this

This moodboard combines lace with 1940s silhouettes

Creating a moodboard helps you to organise and develop your ideas visually. It's a bit like a pinboard on which you display pictures of your favourite things.

- A moodboard is usually developed and presented on a large-format piece of card or board using pins to move things around. You can also use computer design software to create a digital moodboard.

- To build your vintage moodboard, you first need to **choose the period, designer or type of clothing** that interests you. Consider your research and review your sketchbooks to identify what has attracted you most.

- Once you have your theme, **look for connections** between the things you like and select a few images or sketches that represent them. Set these side by side to **explore which combination works best**.

- Think about key words that you might add to **describe your theme**. Is there an appropriate font or style of graphics to use for writing these words on each moodboard?

- **Textures, or even fabric,** may be relevant if you have access to these. For example, you might add a particular button or a bag of sequins to your board.

- Ultimately the moodboard you build needs to inspire you. **Move elements around** and style your selection until you are happy with it.

Creating a new look

Now you have the tools to draw historical fashion, you can put together your own vintage looks. Experiment by mixing and matching elements from different periods to inspire new ideas. The drawings on the opposite page suggest some combinations to get you started.

Fashion designers are often inspired by the past. Think about the ways in which contemporary designs quote, adapt and bring historical styles up to date.

How do you create something original from the past?

- Your aim is to create a design that matches the **mood of the moment**. Sometimes a **fresh interpretation** of a vintage garment is a good way to express the present.
- Try to connect the vintage ideas you like with **contemporary events**. Research what is happening in the world around you – new scientific discoveries, the economy, social changes, popular culture.

Which items should you mix and match?

- First, consider your **favourite vintage designs** – whether a Victorian shirtwaister or a 1960s mini-skirt. How can you incorporate these in a 21st-century fashion collection?
- Think about the **building blocks** of a fashion collection – large items such as coats, jackets and dresses – and start with these.
- Another approach is to begin with key separates – skirts, trousers and tops. Alternatively, think about the **garments worn on the top half of the body** first.
- Isolate the elements you like in your **sketchbook**. Pin these on your **moodboard** (see page 89). Combine them with **images you have found**. Move around ideas until you are ready to design.

How do you develop your designs?

- To develop your designs, take your **moodboard themes, ideas** and **colour palette** and work on the **outline of your collection**.
- Turn your page sideways to sketch **three or four drawings in a row**. As the drawings progress, you will be able to develop each one from the drawing before.
- Think about **silhouette, form, balance, proportion** and **materials**. Subtle tweaks can have a surprising impact.
- Redraw the ideas you like. Try to add **modern accessories** or **combine separates** in surprising ways.
- Share your ideas with friends and tutors to **get feedback**. What they say may help you develop your collection in a new direction.

Circular skirt, 1980s T-shirt

Hot pants, punk sweater

Strapless cocktail dress over a T-shirt

Utility dress, denim jacket

Victorian blouse, flares

Chanel jacket, T-shirt, cropped trousers

Flapper dress, boyfriend cardigan, boots

Art Deco sweater, mini-skirt, sneakers

A good knowledge of fabrics and how they perform will add authenticity to your vintage drawings. The variety of textiles used in clothing is vast. Here is a list of the most familiar types.

Fabrics can be woven, knitted or felted. Note that for woven materials there are three key weaves: plain weave, twill weave and satin weave. Each gives the fabric a different texture.

For suggestions on how to draw different materials, see pages 28–29.

boiled wool
Knitted and felted wool that is washed in hot water and dried a number of times to create a distinctive matte texture. Used for jackets, cardigans and mittens.

bouclé
Warm, textured, woollen fabric that became popular in the 1950s. It has a surface of exposed loops or bobbles of yarn. Used for coats, jackets, skirts and sweaters.

brocade
A traditional silk weave that uses additional wefts (the threads that go across the fabric) to create a raised pattern or decorative design. It is often used in evening wear. Gold, silver or metallic threads may be used to add glamour.

calico
One of the oldest known fabrics. In the UK, the term refers to plain cotton cloth. In the USA, it refers to printed cotton, often with a small floral design or other pattern.

cambric
A fine, sheer cotton used for tops and dresses as well as lingerie. Originally of fine linen, it can also be made of fine wool, silk, polyester or cotton blends. Also called *batiste*.

cashmere
A luxurious wool fibre from the undercoat hair of the Kasmir goat. It is used in fine knitwear, shawls and coats.

chambray
Lightweight cotton material, with one colour as the warp (lengthwise) threads and a white weft. Often resembles denim in colour. It is named after its birthplace, Cambrai in France.

chenille
Chenille has a downy, tufted surface named after the French word for caterpillar (*chenille*). It is used for cardigans, scarves and hats, usually in cotton.

chevron
Material with a V-shaped pattern or print in the weave. It is commonly used for suits or coats.

chiffon
Originally made of silk, chiffon is a light, almost see-through material that drapes beautifully in flowing dresses and tops. It is now commonly made from rayon or polyester as well as silk.

chintz
Plain-weave cotton that is printed and glazed, with heat and pressure, to create a shiny surface. Often designed in bright colours or with floral patterns.

corduroy
Corduroy is woven with an extra weft to create ridges, ribs, cords or wales (vertical ridges) along the length of the fabric. Corduroy was used for men's outdoor clothes and workwear in the first half of the 20th century, and became fashionable for women in the 1960s.

cotton
Yarn made from the fibres of cotton plants grown in Africa, the Americas and India.

crêpe
Woven material with a crinkled surface and stretchy feel. Wool crêpe is commonly used in tailored trousers, skirts, jackets and dresses. See also **georgette**.

crêpe de chine
A thin, fine dress fabric, woven with silk, that has a slightly crinkled texture.

denim
Strong, hard-wearing cloth, traditionally cotton with a twill weave. Originally used for workwear but now commonly associated with jeans.

devoré
A velvet fabric with a semi-translucent pattern, created by burning away the velvet pile with chemicals.

dogstooth
See **houndstooth**.

felt
Fabric of variable density made by matting and bonding fibres together. Usually created from wool and commonly used for hats.

flannel
Soft cotton or wool cloth with a brushed, slightly raised surface. It can be a plain or twill weave and is used for dresses and skirts but also underwear and pyjamas.

gabardine
A tightly woven, durable cloth used for trench coats, windbreakers, uniforms and hard-wearing suits. Gabardine was traditionally made from worsted wool, but is now commonly woven from rayon and cotton.

gauze
Light, translucent cloth, with warps that cross and un-cross. Used for loose, unstructured tops, dresses and skirts. It can be made from silk, wool, cotton or rayon.

georgette
Also called crêpe georgette, this sheer, matte fabric has a crêpe texture created from twisted yarns that add weight. It drapes easily and is used for evening wear.

grosgrain
Tightly woven, fine-ribbed fabric used as a firm ribbon as well as a facing and waistband to join bodices to skirts.

herringbone
Herringbone has a V-shaped woven pattern, also called broken twill. See also **twill weave**.

houndstooth
Two-tone fabric with a lozenge-shaped checked pattern. Used for suits, coats and sportswear. Usually made from tweed in black and white, the pattern is also called dogstooth, or 'puppytooth' for small checks.

jersey
Soft and stretchy machine-knitted fabric that is great for draping. Jersey was first used with wool yarn for sportswear. It is now made from cotton (especially for T-shirts) or from synthetic fibres.

lace
Highly patterned delicate cloth with open holes that create a web-like texture. Lace was traditionally made from linen, silk or precious metal threads, but cotton and synthetic fibres became common in the 20th century.

lamé
Woven or knitted fabric featuring fine metallic yarns. Lamé was used in the 1960s to create a 'space-age' look. It is used for evening and dress wear as well as for glamorous knits.

linen
Both a fabric and a fibre made from the flax plant. Linen cloth is usually plain weave and is used in tops, skirts, dresses and summer suits.

lurex
The metallic-coated yarns incorporated in lamé (see **lamé**), or fabric made from these yarns.

Lycra
The trade name of a man-made elasticised fabric, invented in the 1960s, that is stretchy and flexible. Known as elastane in Europe and spandex in the USA, it is used in figure-hugging dresses, tops, leggings and sportswear.

mohair
Yarn made of lustrous fibres from the hair of the Angora goat. Often woven with wool or cotton, mohair has a fuzzy texture. Popular in the 1950s, it is found in jackets, coats, skirts and sweaters.

moiré
A wavy or watermark pattern on fabric such as taffeta. Created through clever weaves or engraved rollers, it is also called watered silk. It is used to create effect on dresses and trimmings.

muslin
Plainly woven cotton fabric in a variety of weights, usually undyed or white. Used in shirts and dresses. See also calico.

nylon
The first wholly synthetic fibre. Used to create nylon tights at the end of the 1930s and for lingerie, linings and sportswear.

organdie (also organdy)
A fine, sheer and stiff fabric traditionally made from cotton. Used for collar and cuff trims, as well as evening dresses and bridalwear.

organza
A sheer, crisp plain-weave dress fabric traditionally woven from silk. Used for evening dresses, bridalwear, dresses and tops.

pinstripe
Fine thread-like stripes on woven or printed fabric. Associated with business suits.

polyester
Man-made fibres used to create a strong, washable synthetic fabric. Produced under a variety of trade names since 1953, polyester was popular in the 1960s and 1970s for tops, skirts and dresses.

poplin
Finely ribbed medium- to heavy-weight cloth in a plain weave. Originally woven with a silk warp and a wool weft, cotton poplin became more common in the 20th century and is used for dresses, shirts and sportswear.

Prince of Wales
A large, fine check used for light, woollen suit fabric. Usually woven in black and white, or reddish brown and cream, it first became popular in the 1930s when worn by British royalty.

rayon
Artificial silk fibre man-made from cellulose or wood pulp. Invented at the end of the 19th century, rayon is used in tops, dresses, trousers and skirts.

sateen
Cotton fabric with a satin weave that has a smooth, glossy appearance. Used in dresses, skirts and jackets.

satin weave
A type of weave in which the warp (lengthwise) yarns are more visible than the weft, which gives a smooth, shiny feel. Satin also refers to fabric made in this weave from silk, polyester and rayon. It is used for evening or special-occasion wear. See also **sateen**.

seersucker
Woven stripy cotton fabric. The warp yarns are held at different tensions to create alternating smooth and crinkled stripes. Used in summer dresses and blouses.

serge
A twill weave with a diagonal design traditionally associated with navy blue worsted. Serge is also made from wool blends and used in dresses, suits and coats.

shantung
Medium-weight silk fabric with a beautiful sheen and distinctive uneven yarns. Used for smart tailored jackets and trousers as well as full special-occasion dresses.

silk
Made from the unwound cocoon of the silkworm, silk is a strong, lustrous fibre used to make yarn and fabric.

taffeta
Silk taffeta, a plain weave of yarn-dyed silk, has a smooth, sheeny feel and rustles crisply when it moves. Used in ball gowns and bridalwear.

tartan
Woollen twilled cloth with a variety of distinctive plaid designs against a coloured background. Some patterns can identify particular Scottish clans.

tulle
Lightweight hexagonal mesh or netting used for dress and hat trimmings as well as for bridal gowns.

tweed
Coarse textured woollen fabric, traditionally woven near the River Tweed in the Scottish Borders but also associated with Ireland. Different coloured fibres are twisted together to create distinctive shades.

twill
Woven fabric with diagonally ribbed designs, usually made from wool and used in skirts and jackets. See also **gabardine**, **serge**, **tartan** and **denim**.

twill weave
One of the three basic textile weaves, twill can be identified by its distinct diagonal pattern. This is created by weaving the weft yarns over two or more of the warp yarns at regular intervals.

velvet
Woven and tufted fabric, originally made from silk, with a distinctive dense pile. Velvet is used as a trim on daywear as well as for evening or special-occasion clothing.

voile
Meaning 'veil' in French, voile is both sheer and crisp due to the tight twist of the yarns. It can be made of silk, cotton, wool or manufactured fibres. It is used for blouses, dresses and lingerie.

viscose
A man-made fibre, rayon viscose is created from wood pulp. Used to make trousers, skirts and dresses.

wool
Wool is one of the oldest fabrics in the world and is made of fibres originating from the hair of sheep, goats and other animals.

worsted
A woollen fabric woven from tightly twisted yarn that has been made from longer fibres. It has a smoother appearance than other woollens – see also **gabardine** and **serge**.

Many fashion terms derive from French words. This is because Paris was at the centre of the world's fashion industry for much of the 20th century.

For an explanation of textiles, see pages 92–93.

accessories
The items that help to create the overall look of an outfit or design, such as belts, jewellery and scarves.

asymmetrical
When the left and right sides of a design do not match.

Ballets Russes
Influential ballet company, created by Sergei Diaghilev in 1909, famous for its modern music, dancers, choreography, artistic costume and sets.

batwing sleeve
A long sleeve that is wide at the shoulder, with a very deep armhole, and narrows towards the wrist.

bias cut
Fabric cut across the grain to give it stretch and movement.

bodice
The top part of a dress, from the neck to the waist.

body-con
Body-skimming or body-conscious clothing popular in the 1980s and 1990s.

bolero
A cropped open jacket or top, influenced by a style of jacket worn by Spanish men.

brassière
Commonly known as a 'bra', the brassière is an undergarment designed to support the bust.

brief
The practical and creative guidelines for a designer to follow.

bust
A woman's breasts, or the part of a garment that covers them.

bustier
A tight-fitting, usually strapless, waist-length top designed to push up the bust.

bustline
The outline of the bust at its widest part.

cheongsam
Close-fitting style of dress originating in China.

cloche
From the French word for 'bell', a close-fitting hat that curves neatly around the head.

collage
Artistic term for organising and sticking different materials together on one piece of work.

collar
Part of a garment that is usually attached to the neckline.

collection
A selection of designs that work together for a particular season. They often share a key theme, colour or shape.

contemporary
Designs from the present day that feel modern and new.

corsage
A three-dimensional floral detail in a design, or a small bouquet worn as a brooch or bracelet.

corset
A stiff, tight-fitting garment that defines the waistline and shapes the bust and hips. Usually worn as underwear.

couture
The most expensive form of fashion design, with unique garments created for individual clients. The name comes from the French term *haute couture* or 'high-dressmaking'. In Italy it's known as *alta moda*.

croquis
Pronounced 'crow-key'. A figure sketch with elongated proportions used to present fashion designs. It comes from the French word for 'sketch'.

cuff
The detail at the end of a sleeve.

dart
A fold of fabric, sewn into a garment to create shape around the body. It is often used at the bust, waist and hips.

double-breasted
Two rows of buttons on a jacket or coat front, with a wide overlap of fabric.

draping
The skilled process of transforming two-dimensional designs into three-dimensional patterns by hanging cloth on a mannequin.

embroidery
Decorative stitching on fabric with attractive yarns and elaborate patterns or images.

epaulette
A decorative strap on the shoulder of a garment, associated with military uniform.

fashion figure
A drawing of the human form used by a designer to present design ideas. A human is seven and a half heads tall, but a fashion figure is usually at least nine heads tall.

fishnet
An open mesh fabric resembling netting. Used for stockings or tights.

flares
Trousers with legs that widen and open outwards below the knee.

garçonne
Term used to describe young independent women in the 1920s. It was inspired by a contemporary French novel of the same name by Victor Margueritte.

hairline
Where the top of the forehead meets the scalp, or the point where hair grows.

halter neck
A sleeveless garment with straps that meet at the back of the neck.

haute couture
See **couture**.

hem
The edge of a garment created when fabric is folded and sewn under. It often refers to the bottom of a skirt or trousers.

kilt
A pleated wraparound skirt, traditionally worn in Scotland and made of tartan fabric.

lapel
Part of a coat, jacket or shirt that lies below the collar and is folded back on either side of the neckline or opening. Also known as a rever.

LBD
Shorthand term for 'Little Black Dress', usually a short, simple cocktail or evening dress.

matelot
Meaning 'sailor', the term refers to nautically styled clothing, from striped sweaters to buttoned trousers.

mini-dress
A short dress that does not reach the knee.

neckline
The opening for the head on a garment. It often has a device to widen it, such as buttons or a zip, so the head can fit through.

Perspex
Hard transparent plastic, also known as acrylic glass. Used in accessories from the 1960s onwards.

placket
The column of fabric where buttons and buttonholes are found on a shirt or jacket. It can also mean the opening at the neck, sleeve or waist of a garment.

pleat
Fabric folds that add and control fullness in clothing.

portfolio
A selection of a designer's work – illustrations, designs, moodboards – in a folder or digital presentation that shows their research process, design skills and style.

power suit
Wide-shouldered and tailored women's business clothing, associated with the 1980s.

prêt-à-porter
A French term meaning 'ready to wear'. See **ready-to-wear**.

PVC
Abbreviation of polyvinyl chloride – a man-made material used in both clothing and accessories to give a shiny, waterproof finish and to imitate leather and rubber.

raglan sleeve
Type of sleeve with a diagonal seam from the armhole to the neck.

ready-to-wear
Clothing made and sold in standard sizes. It was originally introduced by couture houses in the 1960s as a cheaper alternative to couture, but it now applies to designer clothes as well as high-street brands.

rever
See **lapel**.

rib knit
Vertical stripes or ribs in knitwear used for edgings. Created by alternating a knit and purl stitch in each row.

rockabilly
Youthful fashion style from the 1950s linked to American popular music: rock 'n' roll and country or 'hillbilly'.

shift dress
Uncomplicated above-the-knee dress, usually fitted at the bust with a gently flared skirt.

shirtwaist
A button-down women's blouse popular from the late 19th century onwards. Worn tucked into a long skirt, the look developed into the shirtwaister or shirt dress of the 20th century.

silhouette
The shape created by a garment.

single-breasted
One row of buttons, usually on a jacket or coat front.

sportswear
Less formal 20th-century clothing associated with watching sport or, from the 1930s, worn to attend informal social occasions.

storm flaps
Extra material at the shoulders of a trench coat or a jacket, originally designed to protect the coat opening from adverse weather.

template
An outline fashion figure, or **croquis**, traced over by a designer to speed up the process of creating new designs.

topstitching
A line of stitching on the outside of a garment.

turtleneck
A sweater or T-shirt with a high, tight neck that can also be turned over.

Utility
The British Board of Trade introduced Utility designs for clothing during World War II. These designs used less fabric than traditional clothing designs.

vintage
Vintage fashion traditionally refers to couture or high-quality garments that were made in the past. Today it is used for most second-hand clothing.

waistband
The band of fabric that fits around the waistline of a garment, for example to finish off the top of a skirt or trousers.

waspie belt
Also called a waist cincher or waspie 'corset' (see **corset**), this wide belt pulls in the waist to add curves and definition to an outfit.

yoke
The shaped part of a garment, often around the neck and shoulders, that supports looser pieces of the garment.

INDEX

ACKNOWLEDGMENTS

The authors would like to thank everyone who has contributed to this book, in particular: the designers and fashion experts who have generously shared their ideas, inspiration and images; the team at the Fashion and Textile Museum and Newham College London – Ali, Anna, Carys, Chris, Julia, Melissa, Rajet, Suki and Tareque, along with Dominic Fenton and David and Grace Wilkinson; editor Diana Craig, designer Simon Webb and illustrator Jenny Bowers; commissioning editor Jane Wilsher, production controller Rachel Heley, picture researcher Maria Ranauro, Carolyn Jones and all the staff of Thames & Hudson Ltd.

IMAGE CREDITS

Every effort has been made to contact copyright holders. Any omissions are inadvertent and will be corrected in future editions if notification is given to the publisher in writing. We are grateful to the owners and the following copyright holders who have kindly agreed to make their images available in this book.
2, 18 (left), 19, 44, 47, 53 Norman Parkinson Ltd/Courtesy Norman Parkinson Archive; 6, 7 Anna Sui Corp, 2013; 14 (top left) The Granger Collection/TopFoto; 14 (top right) Marka/SuperStock; 14 (left) Fashion and Textile Museum; 15 (bottom left) Warner Bros/Everett Collection/Rex Features; 15 (top right) Stapleton Collection/Corbis; 15 (bottom right) Copyright Prada; 16 (top right), 18 (top right) Bettmann/Corbis; 16 (left), 17(top left), 17 (bottom/detail) Kerry Taylor Auctions Ltd; 17 (top right) Dennis Nothdruft; 20 (left) Sir Paul Smith by James Mooney; 20 (top right), 21, 56 Marion Foale and Sally Tuffin; 22 (left) TopFoto/UPP; 22 (right), 23 (left and bottom) Bill Gibb; 23 (top right) Justin de Villeneuve; 24, 25, 69, 83 Kirstin Sinclair; 32 (right), 70, 79 David Sassoon; 32 (left) Michael Pick; 61 Chris Barham/Associated Newspapers/Rex Features; 64 Clive Arrowsmith for Zandra Rhodes; 73 Horrockses; 89 Suki Gill.
Throughout: step-by-step/croquis line drawings by Dennis Nothdruft © 2014 Dennis Nothdruft; Line drawings of garments and decorative illustrations © 2014 Jenny Bowers. On the cover front and back: figure and line drawings by Dennis Nothdruft; illustrations by Jenny Bowers.

How to draw vintage fashion © 2014 Thames & Hudson Ltd, London
Text © 2014 Celia Joicey
Step-by-step artwork © 2014 Dennis Nothdruft

Designed by Simon Webb

First published in 2014 in paperback in the United States of America by Thames & Hudson Inc., 500 Fifth Avenue, New York, New York 10110

thamesandhudsonusa.com

Library of Congress Catalog Card Number 2014932778

ISBN 978-0-500-65037-0

Printed and bound in China by Toppan Leefung Printing Limited